Ozema LeDee

DEDICATION

This publication is dedicated to my mother, Leora Mae LeDee Weiloch. To her, I express my gratitude for her inspiration and continued support in making this project a reality. She has contributed to this chronicle by sharing some of her childhood memories and is the very reason that this publication has been researched, compiled and written.

With sincere warmth and appreciation.

Your daughter,

Phyllis Pitre Lastrapes

May 8, 2018

PREFACE

It is important that to know who you are, you must know where you come from. Thus begins the exploration into the lineage of **Ozema Le'Dee** who was born on Saturday, February 28, 1903. Although deceased at the time of this publication, my maternal grandfather, (**Ol' Dad**), lived a long and productive life. For some people, he was simply known as **"Zem."** For others he was affectionately referred to as "**Ol' Dad."** For this narrative, both names are used to refer to **Ozema Le'Dee.** He was a tremendously industrious and creative individual who passed away only seven weeks short of his 102nd birthday, on January 4th, 2005.

Ozeme Ledee

in the U.S., Social Security Death Index, 1935-2014

Name:	Ozeme Ledee
Last Residence:	70570 Opelousas, Saint Landry, Louisiana, USA
BORN:	28 Feb 1903
Died:	4 Jan 2005
State (Year) SSN issued:	Louisiana (Before 1951)

Genealogy, the study and investigation into one's family ancestry, is an arduous, intriguing yet gratifying undertaking. This exploration begins with **Ol' Dad** and proceeds back to his parents, grandparents, etc. until we reach his sixth-great grandparents. At this writing, approximately ten generations will benefit by learning the brief history of these individuals whose lives began in the 1600's.

TABLE OF CONTENTS

INTRODUCTION

The following is a compilation of research performed to trace the ancestry of my maternal grandfather, **Ozema Le'Dee**, along with his spouses who proceeded him in death. Beginning with the most current documentation, this narrative then travels backward to earlier generations.

In addition to a basic narrative disclosing the information located, documentation confirming this information is attached. The reader must be aware that mistakes and discrepancies within documents are inevitable. For example, census enumerators often recorded surnames phonetically. Catholic priests spelled names in French or Spanish depending on their own origin. Also, many at the time, were not given the opportunity for even a remedial education, and therefore were not able to read or write well.
For example, the first names and surnames were often spelled in various ways. I will note such differences in this chronicle. For example, the surname **LeDee**, has been spelled as **LeDe', Ladet, Leday,** and **Ledet.** Historically, surnames evolved to sort people into groups. This categorization can be by occupation, place of origin, clan affiliation, patronage, parentage, adoption, and even physical characteristics (like red hair). Many of the modern surnames in the dictionary can be traced back to Britain and Ireland.

In addition to misspelled names, there are discrepancies in other areas of research. Ages and dates may not always prove to be calculated accurately. As the researcher, I will attempt to bring this information to light as this narrative develops. Childhood memories and/or interviews from living descendants may also prove amusing, as well as interesting to the reader.

Each of us has two parents, two sets (four individuals) of grandparents, four sets (eight individuals) of great grandparents, eight sets (sixteen individuals) of great-great-grandparents, and great-great-great parents have sixteen sets or 32 individuals, in our individual lineage. The further back research progresses, the larger the number of direct ancestors can be found. Again, the focus of this report is on my maternal line;

that of my mother, **Leora Mae Le'Dee's** father, **Ozema.** His lineage was investigated, and information is provided here on several of his direct progenitors.

Because **Ozema** has French and Spanish progenitors, he would be considered a Creole of color. Historically, Creoles of color were/are a historic ethnic group of people that developed in the former French and Spanish colonies of Louisiana. French colonists in Louisiana originally used the term "Creole" to refer to whites born in the colony, rather than those born in France. It was also used for slaves born in the colony, before our country formed states.

CREOLE COMMUNITIES

The report here begins in Louisiana, and many of **Ozema's** descendants have remained in the state as well as in the area near Eunice and the town of Mallet. Prior to the founding of this country, the **Le'Dee's** migrated from Canada, then from France.

All his life, **Zem** lived in St. Landry Parish, Louisiana. St. Landry Parish has a significant population of Creoles, especially in Opelousas and its surrounding areas. The traditional Creole heritage is prevalent in Opelousas, Palmetto, Lawtell, Eunice, Swords, Mallet, Frilot Cove, and many other villages, towns, and communities. The French-Creole language and the Roman Catholic Church are dominate features of this culture.

Church records such as christenings, marriages, and burials, proved invaluable in the area of family history research. It is the goal of the researcher to make this information factual, revealing, historical, and somewhat thought-provoking.

For this chronicle, I, the researcher used *FamilySearch.com* and *Ancestry.Com*, websites, as well as the *Louisiana State Archives, Louisiana State University Library, and the EBR Parish Genealogy Library,* to acquire the information contained here. Other sources investigated were United States, "*Find A Grave*" 1600's to current, Louisiana census enumerations from 1940, 1930, 1920, 1910, 1900, 1880, 1870, and 1850, 1840, 1830, 1820, etc. and the U.S. *Draft Registration Records* from World War I and World War II. The 1890 census was destroyed at the federal level and is therefore inaccessible for public use.

The most current census information available in the United States, is the 1940 enumeration. Due to confidentiality issues, these records must be 75 years old before the public can obtain access. Documents outlining the source(s) of the information are contained in this record, so the reader will have knowledge as to how this information was gathered.

OZEMA'S VENTURES

As an adult, **Zem** had a green dinosaur on a Sinclair Company Oil sign on his property **Zem** was quoted as saying, "I had three places, (operational businesses) and I was running up and down the road all day!" Then he reported, (because of his exhaustion,) "I feel as though I am in the pen (penitentiary), and I didn't kill nobody, so I quit!"

At the age of 93, he finally decided to sell his burial, vault, and monument business to his son **David.** He operated **LeDee's Garage** for over 25 years. The vault business remains on the property where the *Sinclair Company Oil* sign once stood. It should be known that **Zem** was a trailblazer, entrepreneur, and innovator. Among his accomplishments, he could fly a Piper Cub, and land the plane in the field. The plane was an American light aircraft that was built between 1937 and 1947 by *Piper* Aircraft. The aircraft has a simple, lightweight design which gives it good low-speed handling properties and short-field performance. The *Piper* Super *Cub* has been considered by many to be the ultimate backcountry airplane. The *Cub* is one of the best-known light aircraft of all time.

Zem & a friend at LeDee's Garage

To add to his list of skills**, Ol' Dad** also designed and built water pumps. It was reported that because of his ingenuity, and as a man of color, he was nearly 'run off his property" as an act of retaliation.

One of the most recent pieces of data related to my maternal grandfather, **Ol' Dad** was discovered in the *U.S. Social Security Applications and Claims Index 1936-2007.* According to this record, **Ozene Ledee (Ozema Ledee**) *Male, Black, Birthdate 28 May 1903,* (reported in error) *Birthplace Mallet, Louisiana, and he Died 4 January 2005.* It is reported that his *burial* is in *Lawtell, St. Landry Parish, Louisiana, USA* at *St. Anne's Catholic Church.* **Ol' Dad** was baptized Catholic on *April 7, 1903.* His godparents were **Victor Lede'** and **Ulyssia Gobert.**

OZEMA'S EARLY DAYS

Recorded on his baptismal document**, Ol' Dad's** father is listed as **Severan Ledee** and his mother as **Theresa Richard**. On his baptismal document, **Victor Lede'** and **Ulyssia Gobert** were selected as his godparents.

Certificate of Baptism

St. Anthony of Padua Catholic Church
P.O. Box 31
Eunice, Louisiana 70535

This is to Certify

That Ozeimé Ledé
Child of Casimir Ledé
and Theresia Richard
Born in Eunice, La.
on the 28 day of February 19 1903 was

Baptized

on the 7 day of April 19 1903
according to the
Rite of the Roman Catholic Church
by the Rev. Alfred Bacciochi
the Sponsors being Victor Ledé
Ulyssia Gobert
as appears from the Baptismal Register of this Church
Dated 2-9-10 Volume 4 Page 76 No. 80
Seal Rev. Gilbert Dutel Pastor
Per Deacon Gary Goudeau

It is also maintained that **Ozema/Ozeme** is a *United States* citizen whose last residence was *70570* in *St. Landry Parish, Louisiana, USA*. Social Security issued his social security number prior to 1951.

The **Opelousas Daily World** captured the ingenuity and tenacity of **Ol' Dad** in the newspaper's special edition entitled, *Senior World*. It was on 14 March 2004, that the periodical interviewed and discussed how retirees wanted to remain purposeful, involved, and physically active. Those who knew **Zem** stated that he was accomplished, gregarious, and a jack-of-all trades. My grandfather was also very adventurous! Such was **Ol' Dad's** legacy. Thus, he is leaving for us knowledge of how he lived his life, with the anticipation that his essence will encourage, motivate, and inspire his remaining descendants to become involved, resourceful, and independent individuals.

Additionally, the published article in *Senior World* stated that "**LeDee** is an entrepreneur who has excelled in mechanics, music, and education." Others recall that **Ol' Dad** also enjoyed gambling, hunting quail, and making moonshine. At one time, in 1964 **Zem LeDee** and **the Lawtell Playboys** provided entertainment at various venues. **Zem** played the accordion, fiddle, and harmonica. According to his son-in-law **Edwin Marshall,** "He was good at everything, but not farming."

Senior World

Opelousas, Louisiana — Sunday, March 14, 2004

Don't fence them in

Retirees head to wide open spaces

WASHINGTON (AP) — Sunshine and warm temperatures aren't the only lures for retirees. They also want cheaper housing and some elbow room, and that has made places like Colorado, Idaho, Utah and New Mexico increasingly attractive to the over-65 set.

Each of those states saw its senior population grow by at least 6 percent between 2000 and 2003, placing them among the 10 fastest-growing states for that age group, according to Census Bureau figures being released Wednesday.

Much of the growth is due to active retirees from California who go looking for destinations with four-season climates, less congestion and cheaper living costs, said William Frey, a demographer at the Brookings Institution, a Washington think tank.

"What's happening is that baby boomers who moved to California are just now reaching retirement age," Frey said. "California is really sort of a bubbling population of elderly ready to escape high housing costs."

A separate 2002 census survey found the median home value in California was above $275,000, compared with $199,000 in Colorado and $116,000 in New Mexico.

Nevada, which leads the nation in most population growth categories, is tops among the 65-and-over crowd as well. That

See Retirees Page 11

Ozema "Zim" LeDeé of Mallet recently celebrated his 101st birthday.

Photo by Alain A. de la Villesbret

LeDeé a renaissance man

By Alain A. de la Villesbret

MALLET — Ozema "Zim" LeDeé of Mallet is a modern renaissance man. He is an entrepreneur who has excelled in mechanics, music and education and he has worked the good earth. He still lives on the same patch of land that he bought in the early 1940s for $1,800 and upon which he built his home, his tool shop and a vocation school for teaching work skills to black veterans returning from World War II.

"He tried to farm, but he wasn't that good at it. He was good at everything else but not farming," said son-in-law Edwin Marshall.

"He was an outlaw too," said son Wilbert "Blackie" LeDeé. One outlet for his father's mechanical design capabilities came courtesy of white lightning bootleggers in St. Landry Parish. LeDeé made the best stills in south Louisiana, Blackie said.

> "There was always music in the house. He got it from his mother and he passed it on to us."
>
> **Marshall LeDeé, 78**
> *The oldest living son*

LeDeé, was born on Feb. 28, 1903, to Casimaire and Thoresa LeDeé of Mallet. He recently celebrated his 101st birthday in his red brick home on U.S. 190 between Lawtell and Mallet. A congratulations letter from NBC weatherman Willard Scott rested on top of a cabinet in the front living room. It praised him for joining an elite number of Americans over 100 years of age.

"I'm a happy man, happy man," he said as he clapped his hands when he was asked about his life.

At his birthday party last week, LeDeé laughed, told stories and played his harmonica. Family members pinned money to his shirt and prepared a feast. He was surrounded by more than a dozen of his 12 children, 47 grandchildren and more than 40 great-grandchildren. Among his offspring are musicians, teachers, law enforcement officers and mechanics.

See LeDeé Page 2

It was in 2003, that numerous family members and friends gathered in celebration of **Ozema LeDee's** 100th birthday at St. Anne's Church Reception Center in Lawtell. While there, he clapped his hands, told stories, and played his harmonica. Although he ambulated with difficulty, he was physically supported to stand upright, where he joyfully arose to dance in celebration of his special day.

In his younger years, **Zem** and his daughter **Leora** enjoyed going to Zydeco dances. She recalls that her father would bring an extra shirt with him to the affair. While there, **Zem** made his rounds asking all the single ladies to join him in a dance. At the time, it was "unladylike" for a woman to ask a man to dance. **Leora** recalls that, "Dad was so wet with perspiration from the dancing, he had to go and get a second (dry) shirt (from the car) during intermission." Once the pair returned home from the affair, **Nan** would ask, "Why is your belt wet?" **Old Dad's** response was that his daughter **Leora,** "Threw him in a ditch!" and deliberately got his belt wet. All the while everyone laughed and knew it was perspiration from his all night of dancing.

Zydeco is translated to mean snap beans from the song "Les haricots sont pas sales." The dance was born in the black Creole communities on the prairies of southwest Louisiana in the 1920's. It is often considered the Creole music of Louisiana. Zydeco was originally sung only in Louisiana French or Creole. Today, musicians sing in English, or in Colonial Louisiana French. One instrument unique to zydeco is a washboard. The washboard is made of corrugated aluminum and played by the musician working bottle caps or spoons up and down the length of the board. Zydeco music also makes use of the accordion that **Zem** played with gusto.

In addition to his love of music, dancing, fishing, hunting quail, and travel to Hot Springs, Arkansas, **Ol' Dad** developed, *"A String of Inventions,"* according to the Opelousas Daily World of *Wednesday, January 27, 1999.* The publication stated that, at age 96, **Zem** maintained his license to drive, and was then involved in mounting a motor on a concrete mixer that he himself constructed. He also built tractors from scratch, pumps to irrigate rice fields to pump the fields dry, a potato digger and grass cutter. According to **Zem,** "The potato digger would shake the dirt off the potato, so the tuber lies on top of the row."

A few of Zem's Patented Inventions

Alain A. de la Villesbret, of the *Opelousas Daily World,* stated that until his death, "**LeDee** lived on the same patch of land that he bought in the early 1940's for $1800.00." It was on this property, that **Ol' Dad** built his home, his tool shop, and a vocational school for training black veterans returning from World War II.

It was in March of 1947, that the *Opelousas Daily World* stated in the newspaper's headline, *Institute Formed To Train Colored Men.* Additionally, it was reported that, "The school will be operated by an institution guided by an advisory committee. Classes have begun, being conducted in the workshop of **Ozema LeDee**, a colored mechanic, located just west of Lawtell. There are 24 colored veterans, (who) are in training with the G.I. Bill of Right funding. Presently, the men are taught, welding, blueprint reading, and one will soon take up blacksmithing." At the inception of the vocational school, the *George W. Carver Institute*, was founded for "training Louisiana colored people in farm mechanics and related trades." Another basis for the institution is the fact that farms were being mechanized, and that small industries were expanding. At the time there was a specific need for skilled farm workers. A group of Opelousas businessmen characterized the venture as filling a "vital need." Businessman **Glen W Madere** stated that, "There are trade schools for training white men, but there is not a single large trade school in Louisiana dedicated to the training of the colored labor supply."

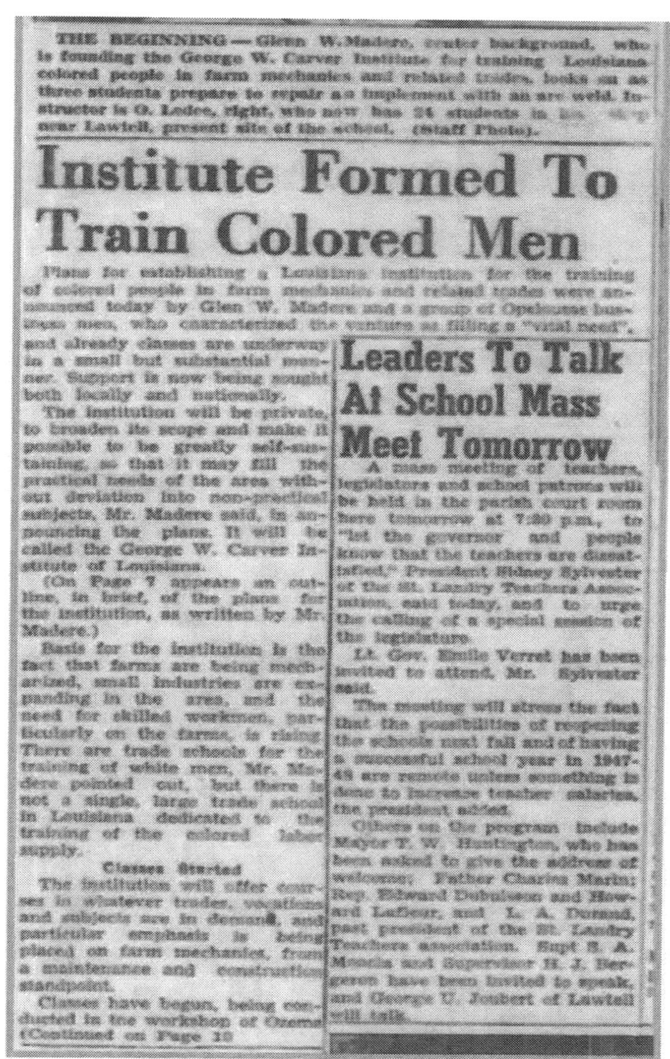

THE BEGINNING — Glenn W. Madere, center background, who is founding the George W. Carver Institute for training Louisiana colored people in farm mechanics and related trades, looks on as three students prepare to repair an implement with an arc weld. Instructor is O. Ledee, right, who now has 24 students in his [illegible] near Lawtell, present site of the school. (Staff Photo).

Institute Formed To Train Colored Men

Plans for establishing a Louisiana institution for the training of colored people in farm mechanics and related trades were announced today by Glen W. Madere and a group of Opelousas business men, who characterized the venture as filling a "vital need", and already classes are underway in a small but substantial manner. Support is now being sought both locally and nationally.

The institution will be private, to broaden its scope and make it possible to be greatly self-sustaining, so that it may fill the practical needs of the area without deviation into non-practical subjects, Mr. Madere said, in announcing the plans. It will be called the George W. Carver Institute of Louisiana.

(On Page 7 appears an outline, in brief, of the plans for the institution, as written by Mr. Madere.)

Basis for the institution is the fact that farms are being mechanized, small industries are expanding in the area, and the need for skilled workmen, particularly on the farms, is rising. There are trade schools for the training of white men, Mr. Madere pointed out, but there is not a single, large trade school in Louisiana dedicated to the training of the colored labor supply.

Classes Started

The institution will offer courses in whatever trades, vocations and subjects are in demand, and particular emphasis is being placed on farm mechanics, from a maintenance and construction standpoint.

Classes have begun, being conducted in the workshop of Ozema

(Continued on Page 10

Leaders To Talk At School Mass Meet Tomorrow

A mass meeting of teachers, legislators and school patrons will be held in the parish court room here tomorrow at 7:30 p.m., to "let the governor and people know that the teachers are dissatisfied," President Sidney Sylvester of the St. Landry Teachers Association, said today, and to urge the calling of a special session of the legislature.

Lt. Gov. Emile Verret has been invited to attend, Mr. Sylvester said.

The meeting will stress the fact that the possibilities of reopening the schools next fall and of having a successful school year in 1947-48 are remote unless something is done to increase teacher salaries, the president added.

Others on the program include Mayor T. W. Huntington, who has been asked to give the address of welcome; Father Charles Marin; Rep. Edward Dubuisson and Howard LaFleur, and L. A. Durand, past president of the St. Landry Teachers association. Supt S. A. Moncla and Supervisor H. J. Bergeron have been invited to speak, and George U. Joubert of Lawtell will talk.

Opelousas Daily World

Thursday, March 13, 1947

It was on July 30, 1952, when the *Opelousas Daily World* bore headlines concerning, "A Dissolution Notice" in the community's newspaper. The publication stated, "Notice is hereby given that the shareholders of the *Lincoln Vocational Institute, Inc.*, have given their unanimous written notice, that this corporation be voluntarily dissolved out of court." It is uncertain as to when the institute altered its name from the *Carver Institute* or if this is a separate property or institution. Nonetheless, the announcement was signed by, **Ozema LeDee.**

Details of the dissolution notice reported that, "**Seth Lewis,** attorney, came before the board with a request that the property of the Old Pot Cove School, now abandoned be sold back to **Severan LeDee (Ozema's** father) at the same price for which the board purchased the property.

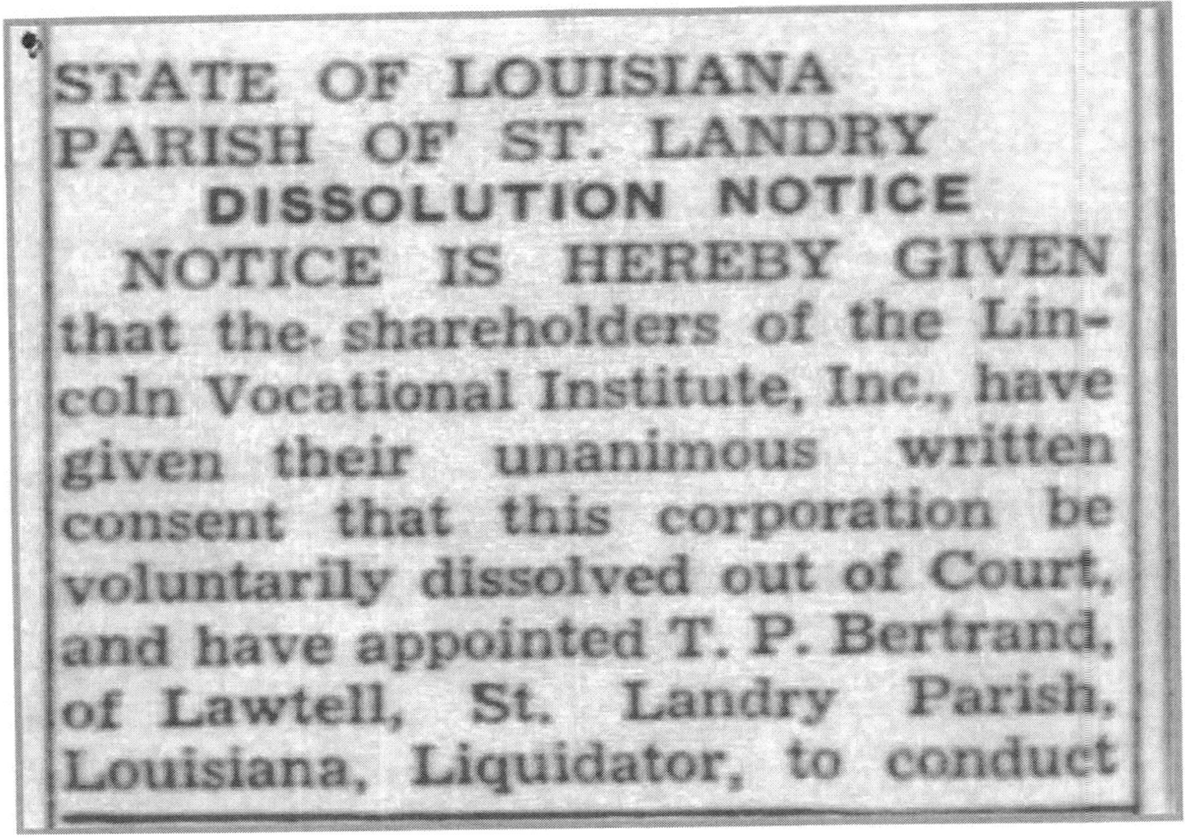

STATE OF LOUISIANA
PARISH OF ST. LANDRY
DISSOLUTION NOTICE

NOTICE IS HEREBY GIVEN that the shareholders of the Lincoln Vocational Institute, Inc., have given their unanimous written consent that this corporation be voluntarily dissolved out of Court, and have appointed T. P. Bertrand, of Lawtell, St. Landry Parish, Louisiana, Liquidator, to conduct

All American men born between February 17, 1887 and/or before December 31, 1921 were required to complete a *World War II Draft Card.* A registration card was completed by **Ozama LeDee** in 1942. At the age of 39, **Ol' Dad** stated that he was *self-employed* in *general repairing* and *welding* in Lawtell. His birthdate is incorrectly reported as *February 18, 1903.* For your review, the registration document is attached. Dated February 14, 1942, the document states that, **Ol' Dad** is *Negro,* with *brown eyes, black hair,* and a *light brown complexion.* Reporting this information is the National Archives at Fort Worth, Texas, *First Registration Draft Cards* which were compiled from 1940-1945.

SERIAL NUMBER	1. NAME (Print)			ORDER NUMBER
T 1708	OZAMA (First)	— (Middle)	LEDEE (Last)	T 10623

2. PLACE OF RESIDENCE (Print)

OPELOUSAS LA ROUTE 4 - #179 ST. LANDRY LA

(Number and street) (Town, township, village, or city) (County) (State)

[THE PLACE OF RESIDENCE GIVEN ON THE LINE ABOVE WILL DETERMINE LOCAL BOARD JURISDICTION; LINE 2 OF REGISTRATION CERTIFICATE WILL BE IDENTICAL]

3. MAILING ADDRESS

Same

(Mailing address if other than place indicated on line 2. If same insert word same)

4. TELEPHONE	5. AGE IN YEARS	6. PLACE OF BIRTH
	# 39	MALLET (Town or county)
	DATE OF BIRTH	
(Exchange) (Number)	FEB. 18 1903 (Mo.) (Day) (Yr.)	LA. (State or country)

7. NAME AND ADDRESS OF PERSON WHO WILL ALWAYS KNOW YOUR ADDRESS

T. P. BERTRAND ROUTE 4 OPELOUSAS, LA

8. EMPLOYER'S NAME AND ADDRESS

SELF Gen. REPAIRING AND WELDING

9. PLACE OF EMPLOYMENT OR BUSINESS

LAWTELL OPELOUSAS ST. LANDRY

(Number and street or R. F. D. number) (Town) (County) (State)

I AFFIRM THAT I HAVE VERIFIED ABOVE ANSWERS AND THAT THEY ARE TRUE.

D. S. S. Form 1 (Revised 1-1-42) (over) ☆ GPO 16-21630-1

Ozema LeDee

(Registrant's signature)

		EYES		HAIR		Light	
Negro	✓	Blue		Blonde		Ruddy	
		Gray		Red		Dark	
Oriental		Hazel		Brown		Freckled	
		Brown	✓	Black	✓	Light brown	✓
Indian		Black		Gray		Dark brown	
				Bald		Black	
Filipino							

Other obvious physical characteristics that will aid in identification..........

I certify that my answers are true; that the person registered has read or has had read to him his own answers; that I have witnessed his signature or mark and that all of his answers of which I have knowledge are true, except as follows:

Fey Durio Lazare
(Signature of registrar)

Registrar for Local Board 2 Opelousas, La
(Number) (City or county) (State)

Date of registration Feb. 14, 1942

Local Board No. 2 44
St. Landry Parish 097
002

United States WWII Draft Cards

Young Men 1940-1947

Continuing to an earlier time, the 1940 *United States Federal Census* reveals that **Ozema Ledet** was a *37-year-old* residing in *St. Landry Parish.* With him are his wife **Frances** *age 28,* and children **Herbert** *age 16*, **Marchal** *14,* **Milbert** *12,* **John** 10, **Lilliana** *8,* **Lellia** *6,* and **Lorilla** *2.* It is also reported that **Ozema** is *male, Negro, born* in *Louisiana, married, head of household,* with a profession as an *automobile mechanic, house is owned*, highest grade completed is the *6th grade.*

Ozema Ledet

in the 1940 United States Federal Census

Name:	Ozema Ledet
Respondent:	Yes
Age:	37
Estimated birth year:	abt 1903
Gender:	Male
Race:	Negro (Black)
Birthplace:	Louisiana
Marital Status:	Married
Relation to Head of House:	Head
Home in 1940:	St Landry, Louisiana
Map of Home in 1940:	View Map
Farm:	No
Inferred Residence in 1935:	Sp, St Landry, Louisiana
Residence in 1935:	Same Place
Resident on farm in 1935:	No
Sheet Number:	14B
Number of Household in Order of Visitation:	219
Occupation:	Automobile Mechanic
Industry:	Lerair Shop
House Owned or Rented:	Owned
Value of Home or Monthly Rental if Rented:	500
Attended School or College:	No
Highest Grade Completed:	Elementary school, 6th grade
Class of Worker:	Working on own account
Weeks Worked in 1939:	52
Income:	0
Income Other Sources:	Yes
Neighbors:	View others on page

Household Members:

Name	Age
Ozema Ledet	37
Frances Ledet	28
Herbert Ledet	16
Marchal Ledet	14
Milbert Ledet	12
John Ledet	10
Lilliana Ledet	8
Lellia Ledet	6
Lorilla Ledet	2

SAVE

LEDEE' & PAPILLION CONNECTIONS

Frances (Nan) Papillion LeDee

Enjoying her flower garden – 1988

Zem's 2nd wife and mother to six of his children**, Frances** passed away on Tuesday November 25, 1997 at Opelousas General Hospital. The Opelousas Daily World and according to Louisiana, *Find a Grave Index,* 1700-2012, **Nan** was born on July 7, 1912. She was 85 years old when she passed away on November 25, 1997 in Opelousas General Hospital.

Frances Ledee

MALLET — Funeral services for Mrs. Frances Papillion Ledee, 85, were held at 10 a.m. Friday in St. Ann Catholic Church here with burial in the church cemetery.

The Rev. Matthew P. Higginbotham conducted the services.

Mrs. Ledee died Tuesday, November 25, 1997, in Opelousas General Hospital.

Survivors include her husband, Ozema Ledee of Lawtell; seven sons, David Ledee, Theme Ledee and Moses Ledee, all of Lawtell, Willard Ledee of Oakland, Calif., Jacob Ledee of Lafayette, Wilbert Ledee and Marshall Ledee, both of Lake Charles; and three daughters, Mrs. Lorella Ledee Marshall of Lawtell, Mrs. Leona Gallow of Beaumont, Texas, and Mrs. Leola Brickman of Chicago, Ill. She also survived by a host of grandchildren; great-grandchildren; great-great-grandchildren; and other relatives and friends.

Mrs. Ledee was preceded in death by two sons, Herbert Ledee and John Ledee.

A wake was held from 5 to 10 p.m. Thursday in Williams Funeral Home in Opelousas, which is in charge of arrangements. A rosary was recited at 7 p.m.

ancestry

Francis "nan" Papillion Ledee'

in the Web: Louisiana, Find A Grave Index, 1700-2012

Name:	Francis "nan" Papillion Ledee'
Birth Date:	7 Jul 1912
Age at Death:	85
Death Date:	25 Nov 1997
Burial Place:	Lawtell, St. Landry Parish, Louisiana, USA

When she married **Zem,** the 24-year-old **Frances** would become mother to six of **Zem's** biological children who had lost their mother a year earlier in an auto accident. Those six children ranged in age from 14 months (**Leora**) to 11 years old (**Herbert**).

On November 19, 1934, **Zem** age 32 (former husband to **Lilly Durosseau**) married **Frances** in St. Landry Parish. **Rev. Julian Vaneyene** a rector at Chataignier, officiated the couple's marriage. Parents listed on their marital document testified that **Nan's** parents were **Matorie Gobert** and **Augustine Papillion.**

Within a year following the death of his first wife **Lilly,** in 1934, **Zem** would take as his bride, **Frances Papillion** (surname translated as butterfly in French) age 24. **Nan** was described as a woman who was gracious, warm, dutiful, thoughtful, hardworking, and devoted to family. According to her headstone, **Frances/Nan** "Gave so much but asked so little." **Nan** treasured vegetable and flower gardening, as well as spending time at home. She especially loved growing roses.

22-0244

STATE OF LOUISIANA
PARISH OF ST. LANDRY

KNOW ALL MEN BY THESE PRESENTS:

THAT WE, Ozeme Ledet, as principal and Adeline Papillon as security, are held and firmly bound unto the Governor of the State of Louisiana in the sum of THREE HUNDRED DOLLARS for the payment of which we bind ourselves, our heirs, executors and administrators, jointly and severally, by these presents.

Dated at Opelousas, this 11th day of November 1935

WHEREAS, a license has been issued by the Clerk of the District Court in and for the Parish of St. Landry, to unite in the Bonds of Matrimony the above bound Ozeme Ledet and Frances Papillon

NOW, THEREFORE, the condition of the above obligation is such, that if there should exist no legal impediment to this alliance, then the above obligation to be null and void; else remain in full force and virtue.

SIGNED IN THE PRESENCE OF

[signature]

Ozeme Ledet
adline Papillion

Color of Man Colored
Age 32 Residence Crowley, La.
Mother Theresa Richard
Residence Mallet
Father Severin Ledet Sr.
Residence Mallet
Former Wife Lillie Dousseau Dead ~~Living~~

Color of Woman Colored
Age 24 Residence Mallet
Mother Matine Guidry
Residence Mallet
Father Augustin Papillon
Residence Mallet
Former Husband none Dead Living

Relationship of contracting parties none

State of Louisiana, Parish of St. Landry

To Any Minister of the Gospel, Judge or Justice of Peace of the Parish of St. Landry—GREETING:

You are hereby authorized and empowered to unite in the Bonds of Matrimony, according to law and established rules,

Mr. Ozemy Ledet
and Miss Frances Papillon

And when you shall have done so, that you certify to same on the reverse hereof, yourself and three witnesses, as required and return within thirty days to the office of the Clerk of the District Court in and for the Parish of St. Landry.

Given under my hand and seal of office, as Clerk of said Court, in and for the Parish of St. Landry the 11th day of November 1935

[signature] Clerk.

STATE OF LOUISIANA
PARISH OF ST. LANDRY

PROCESS VERBAL OF MARRIAGE

THIS IS TO CERTIFY, That I, Rev. Julien Vanuxem, rector Chataignier, have this, the 19 day of November A. D. 1935 united in the Holy Bonds of Matrimony Ozeme Ledet with Francis Papillion. in the presence of the undersigned witnesses.

Ozeme Ledet

Written on the marriage document, it is stated, "That we, **Ozeme Ladet**, as principal and **Adelin Papillion**, as security, are held and firmly bound unto the Governor of the State of Louisiana in the sum of THREE HUNDRED DOLLARS for the payment of which we bind ourselves, our heirs, executors and administrators, jointly and severally, by these presents. Dated at Opelousas, this 17th day of November 1935. Whereas a license has been issued by the Clerk of the ____?___ District Court in and for the Parish of St. Landry, to unite in the Bonds of Matrimony the above bound **Ozeme Ladet** and **Frances Papillion.**" The document continues: Color of Man *colored,* Age, *32,* Residence *Crowley, LA,* Mother ***Theresa Richard,*** Residence *Mallet,* Father, ***Severin Ledet,*** *Sr.*, Residence *Mallet,* Former Wife ***Lillie Durosseau.***

Contained in this publication from 1935 is the marital document which states that, **Ozema's** wife **Frances** is: Color of Woman, *colored,* Age *24,* Residence *Mallet,* Mother ***Matorie Gaubert,*** Residence *Mallet,* Father ***Augustin Papillion,*** Residence *Mallet* and Former husband *none.* **Ozema** and **Frances** married in 1935.

It was during the enumeration of the 1930 United States Census that **Francina Pappallion** was discovered living as a *seventeen-year-old* in the home of her *parents.* Although contained in this chronicle, **Nan's** household consisted of her parents **Augustin**, *age 64* and **Clemontine Pappallion** *age 60.* Additional family members are **Antin Pappallion** *20,* and **Willie Pappallion** *age 15.* According to this report, **Frances** has a *birth year of 1913,* is *Negro, born in Louisiana,* is *single,* and *daughter* of the *head of household.* Both of her parents were *Louisiana born.* Furthermore, **Frances** has *not attended school* and is *unable to read or write.*

Francina Pappallion

in the 1930 United States Federal Census

Name:	Francina Pappallion [Francina Papillion]
Birth Year:	abt 1913
Gender:	Female
Race:	Negro (Black)
Birthplace:	Louisiana
Marital Status:	Single
Relation to Head of House:	Daughter
Home in 1930:	Police Jury Ward 6, St Landry, Louisiana
Map of Home:	View Map
Dwelling Number:	273
Family Number:	277
Attended School:	No
Able to Read and Write:	No
Father's Birthplace:	Louisiana
Mother's Birthplace:	Louisiana
Able to Speak English:	Yes

Household Members:

Name	Age
Augustin Pappallion	64

1930 (continued)

Name	Age
Clemontine Pappallion	60
Antlin Pappallion	20
Francina Pappallion	17
Willie Pappallion	15

Neighbors: View others on page

LEDEE' & DUROSSEAU CONNECTIONS

Ten years prior to the 1940 census and found in the 1930 federal census **Ozema Lede** is *27 years old* employed as a *farmer* on a *general farm.* The couple is *renting* their family home on a *gravel road.* With **Ozema**, are his wife **Lily** age 28, and their three sons **Herbert** *age 6,* **Marshal** *4,* and **Wilbur** *age 1.* The family home, in 1930 is in the *6th Ward* of *St. Landry Parish Louisiana.*

During the fall of 1934, **Zem's** first wife **Lilly Durosseau LeDee,** a sibling, along with her older children attended a church fair. On their return trip to the family's home, all were involved in an automobile accident. The weather conditions were rainy, and the road was slippery. The oldest child **Herbert** sustained a one inch cut below his right eye. Interviews stated that the car was a Model T and the children's mother was sitting in the car's rumble seat. There was an auto crash and **Lilly's** neck was broken. It was reported that she died instantly from the injuries.

Information extracted from *"The New Era"* a Eunice, Louisiana newspaper, reported the following headlines: "One Killed as Cars Collide Near Lawtell." Published Friday, November 23, 1934, the account states that, *"Mamou People Narrowly Escape Death In Sabbath Day Crash-Five Injured.* Additionally,....

"A head on collision of automobiles driven by **Landry Granger** of _?_ who was driving a model ? sedan and Negroes, resulted in instant death of a Negro woman and various injuries to five occupants of the two cars ?. evening on the Eunice-Opelousas Highway between Swords and Lawtell." The publication further reports that, "**Mrs. Onezeme Ledet** came to her death about 3 p.m. on November 18, about two miles west of Lawtell." Details from the publication are contained in this narrative.

Zem was reportedly out of town at the time of the accident. **Lilly's** body was removed from the accident and placed on the family's bed before **Zem** returned home. It was Sunday evening on November 18, 1934. She was 33 years old and left behind a husband, **Ozema,** and their six children.

THE NEW ERA

Eunice, La

Friday November 23, 1934
Single Copy 5 Cents
Subscription $2.00 per year

ONE KILLED AS CARS COLLIDE NEAR LAWTELL

Mamou People Narrowly Escape Death In Sabbath Day Crash - Five Injured

A head on collision of automobiles driven by Landry Granger of ___?___ who was driving a model ___?___ sedan & negroes, resulted in instant death of a negro woman & various injuries to five occupants of the two cars ___?___ evening on the Eunice-Opelousas Highway between Swords sta. Lawtell.

Landry Granger sustained several fractured ribs and an injured leg; and Kelly Fontenot, age 11, respectively who were in the other car, suffered head & abrasions & cuts while their ______?______ was cut about the face. Fontenot's family resides in Ma___. The dead negro woman is said to be a sister of the negro Victor Derousseau, driving the other car. Her name was given as Mrs. Onezeme Ledet. ___?___ negroes are said to have run ___?___ Granger's car as their machine ___?___ considerable along the highway and ___?___ is to Granger's automobile. ___?___ was reported to have been drunk. Injured boys were picked up by J.B. Lewis who was at the scene of the crash. Brought to the Eunice Clinic where their wounds were treated. Granger was also treated at the local hospital.

Mr. Granger's car was badly damaged. The radiator was destroyed, the engine & chassis thrown out of line, and glasses broken. Coroner B.A. Littell's jury composed of Allen McCoy, Amos Bihm, Leon Latiolais, Oscar Bihm and Zenon Joubert rendered the following decision in connection with the tragic accident. We the Coroner's Jury investigated the death of Mrs. Onezeme Ledet, after investigating the case have come to the conclusion that the said Mrs. Onezeme Ledet came to her death about 3 p.m. on Nov. 18, about two miles west of Lawtell in an automobile collision, the driver of the car in which she was killed being Victor Derousseau and the driver of the other car being Landry Granger.

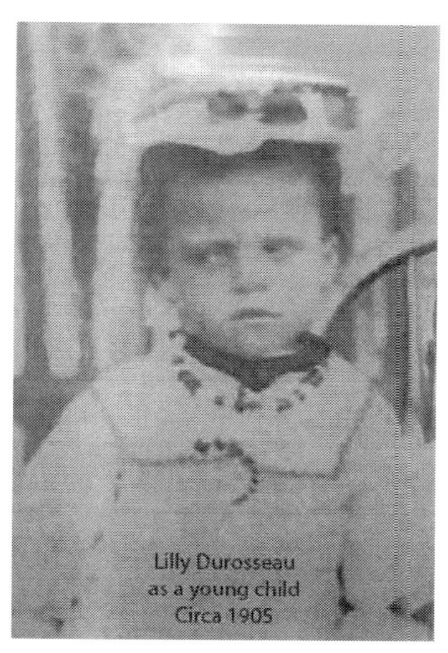
Lilly Durosseau
as a young child
Circa 1905

Lilly Durosseau LeDee

As previously stated, during the census of 1930, **Ozema**, *age 27,* and his wife **Lily** *age 28*, were living in the *6th ward of St. Landry Parish, Louisiana.* Their street address was on a *gravel road* and *dwelling number 288 was their rental home.* The document stated that the family is residing on a *farm.* In the family's home are children **Herbert Lede** age 6, **Marshal Lede** age *4,* and **Wilbur** age 1. It is also reported that the family owns *no radio set,* and both parties can *speak English.* **Ozeme's** parents have Louisiana as their place of birth.

Ozeme Lede

in the 1930 United States Federal Census

Name:	Ozeme Lede
Birth Year:	abt 1903
Gender:	Male
Race:	Negro (Black)
Birthplace:	Louisiana
Marital Status:	Married
Relation to Head of House:	Head
Home in 1930:	Police Jury Ward 6, St Landry, Louisiana, USA
Map of Home:	View Map
Street address:	Gravel
Dwelling Number:	288
Family Number:	301
Home Owned or Rented:	Rented
Radio Set:	No
Lives on Farm:	Yes
Age at First Marriage:	20
Able to Read and Write:	Yes
Father's Birthplace:	Louisiana
Mother's Birthplace:	Louisiana
Able to Speak English:	Yes
Occupation:	Farmer
Industry:	General Farm
Class of Worker:	Working on own account
Employment:	Yes

Household Members:

Name	Age
Ozeme Lede	27
Lily Lede	28
Herbert Lede	6
Marshal Lede	4
Wilbur Lede	1

Neighbors: View others on page

Eleven years earlier, **Zem** and **Lilly's** marriage document from St. Landry Parish courthouse in Opelousas reported:

"When she was about 20 years old, **Lilly Durosseau** a *colored* woman, from *Mallet,* married **Ozema LeDet** age about *20 years old.* According to their marriage license, both parties were residents of *Mallet, Louisiana***.** **Lilly's** parents are listed as **Eva** (aka

Mom TEE FEE) Durosseau and (deceased) **Jean (John) Baptiste Durosseau.** This was the first marriage for both **Ozema** and **Lilly**."

OZEME'S MARRIAGES

10-0278 10-0278

STATE OF LOUISIANA
PARISH OF ST. LANDRY

KNOW ALL MEN BY THESE PRESENTS:

THAT WE Ozeme Ledet as principal and L Durosseau as security, are held and firmly bound unto the Governor of the State of Louisiana in the sum of THREE HUNDRED DOLLARS for the payment of which we bind ourselves, our heirs, executors and administrators, jointly and severally, by these presents.

Dated at Opelousas, this 28 day of May 1923.

WHEREAS, a license has been issued by the Clerk of the District Court in and for the Parish of St. Landry, to unite in the Bonds of Matrimony the above bound Ozeme Ledet and Lilly Durosseau

NOW, THEREFORE, the condition of the above obligation is such, that if there should exist no legal impediment to this alliance, then the above obligation to be null and void; else remain in full force and virtue.

SIGNED IN THE PRESENCE OF

Ozema Ledet
L Durosseau

Color of Man Col	Color of Woman Col
Age 20 Residence Mallet	Age 20 Residence Mallet
Mother Thena Ledet	Mother Eva Durosseau
Residence Mallet	Residence Mallet
Father Simon Ledet	Father Jno Durosseau
Residence Mallet	Residence Dead
Former Wife None Dead Living	Former Husband none Dead Living

Relationship of contracting parties none

State of Louisiana, Parish of St. Landry

To any Judge or Justice of the Peace of the Parish of St. Landry—GREETING:

You are hereby authorized and empowered to unite in the Bonds of Matrimony, according to law and established rules, Mr. Ozeme Ledet and Miss Lilly Durosseau

And when you shall have done so, that you make duplicate acts of the celebration thereof, signed by yourself and three witnesses, as required by law, one of which acts shall return within thirty days to the office of the Clerk of the District Court in and for the Parish of St. Landry, together with this License.

Given under my hand and seal of office, as Clerk of said Court, in and for the Parish of St. Landry the 28 day of May

Ancestry provided a summary of **Francis'** life following this paragraph. This information has not been confirmed by the researcher but may prove helpful and interesting to the reader. This post is in two parts. Part two begins with Nan at age 71.

MISCELLANEOUS PAPILLION INFORMATION

ancestry

Frances (aka NAN) Papillion ledee

BIRTH 7 JULY 1912
DEATH 25 NOVEMBER 1997 • Opelousas, Saint Landry, Louisiana, USA

Facts

Age 0 — **Birth**
7 July 1912

Age 3 — **Birth of Brother Willie Papillion** (1915–1983)
27 Aug 1915 • Louisiana

Age 18 — **Death of Sister Aurelia Papillon** (1890–1930)
1930

Age 29 — **Death of Father Augustin Papillon** (1865–1942)
8Feb1942 • Louisana

Age 31 — **Death of Mother Clementine Gobert** (1870–1944)
9 April 1944 • St Landry , Louisiana, USA

Age 47 — **Death of Sister Amanda Papillion** (1900–1959)
Oct. 25, 1959 • St Landry Parish

Age 49 — **Death of Brother Jimmie Papillon** (1907–1962)
22 Apr 1962 • Texas USA

Age 55 — **Death of Brother Hypolite Paul Papillion** (1892–1968)
Feb. 6, 1968 • Louisana, USA

Age 59 — **Death of Brother Augustin Papillon** (1904–1971)
July 1971 • Beaumont, Jefferson, Texas, United States of America

Age 60 — **Death of Sister Avia Papillion** (1896–1973)
08 Jun 1973 • Church Point, Acadia, Louisiana, USA

Age 63 — **Death of Sister Cora Papillion** (1895–1975)
July 29, 1975 • Church Point, Acadia, Louisiana, United States of America

Sources

Ancestry Sources

Ancestry Family Trees

Family

Parents

Augustin Papillon 1865–1942

Clementine Gobert 1870–1944

Spouse

Age 71 — **Death of Brother Willie Papillion** (1915–1983)
Jul 1983 • Lawtell, Saint Landry, Louisiana, United States of America

Age 75 — **Death of Sister Victoria Papillon** (1899–1987)
5 October 1987 • St Landry , Louisiana, USA

Age 75 — **Death of Brother Adline Papillion** (1909–1988)
feb. 21, 1988 • New Orleans, Orleans, Louisiana, United States of America

Age 85 — **Death**
25 November 1997 • Opelousas, Saint Landry, Louisiana, USA

When **Zem's** second wife **Frances** was about eight years old, in 1920, she is revealed in her family's home with her parents and siblings. According to the report, **Francena Papillion,** was born about 1912 in Louisiana. The census file stated that she is living in *St. Landry Parish, Ward 6.* She is the daughter to **Ogustain Papillion** *age 55,* and **Clementine Papillion** *age 51.* **Frances** is *Mulatto, single, female, able to speak English,* has *attended school,* and is *capable of reading and writing.*

In the home during this 1920 enumeration are **Caror Papillion** age 21, **Amada** 17, **Ogust** 15, **Jammie** 12, **Anthony** 10, and **Frances**' younger brother **Willie,** age 4.

Francena Papillion

in the 1920 United States Federal Census

Name:	Francena Papillion
Age:	8
Birth Year:	abt 1912
Birthplace:	Louisiana
Home in 1920:	Police Jury Ward 6, St Landry, Louisiana
Race:	Mulatto
Gender:	Female
Relation to Head of House:	Daughter
Marital Status:	Single
Father's name:	Ogustain Papillion
Father's Birthplace:	Louisiana
Mother's name:	Papillion
Mother's Birthplace:	Louisiana
Able to Speak English:	Yes
Attended School:	Yes
Able to Read:	Yes
Able to Write:	Yes
Neighbors:	View others on page
Household Members:	

Name	Age
Ogustain Papillion	55

Name	Age
Clementine Papillion	51
Caror Papillion	21
Amada Papillion	17
Ogust Papillion	15
Jammie Papillion	12
Anthony Papillion	10
Francena Papillion	8
Willie Papillion	4

SAVE Cancel

1920 (continued)

Prior to **Frances'** birth, and during the 1910 census, her parents were revealed in the 1910 Louisiana census. The text describes the family of ten members as **Augusta,** *age 50, head of household* in *Mallet, Louisiana.* As head of household, **Nan's** father has an approximate *birth year of 1860* in Louisiana. He is described as *mulatto, head, married,* native tongue *French,* occupation of *farmer,* and *owning his own farm.*

While nine children were born to **Clementine,** *age 38,* one child has not survived to be reported in this enumeration. **Augusta** has *not attended school* and is *unable to read and write.* At the time of this reporting, the couple have been *married for 23 years.*

At the time of this 1910 recording, the **Papillion** family consisted of **Cadar** 18, **Hyt** age 15, **Cora** 14, **Eva** 12, **Victoria** 9, **Amanda** 8, **August** 6, and **Jimmy** age 3. The couple's daughter **Frances (Nan) Zem LeDee's** wife, would not be born until about two years later.

ancestry

Augusta Papillion

in the 1910 United States Federal Census

Name:	Augusta Papillion *[Augustin Peppelion]* [Augusta Peppelion] [Augustas Peppelion]
Age in 1910:	50
Birth Year:	abt 1860
Birthplace:	Louisiana
Home in 1910:	Mallet, Saint Landry, Louisiana
Race:	Mulatto
Relation to Head of House:	Head
Marital Status:	Married
Spouse's Name:	Clementine Papillion
Father's Birthplace:	Louisiana
Mother's Birthplace:	Louisiana
Native Tongue:	French
Occupation:	Farmer
Industry:	Farm
Employer, Employee or Other:	Own Account
Home Owned or Rented:	Own
Home Free or Mortgaged:	Free
Farm or House:	Farm

Attended School:	No
Able to Read:	No
Able to Write:	No
Years Married:	23
Number of Children Born:	9
Out of Work:	N
Number of weeks out of work:	N
Neighbors:	View others on page

Household Members:

Name	Age
Augusta Papillion	50
Clementine Papillion	38
Cadar Papillion	18
Hyt Papillion	15
Cora Papillion	14
Eva Papillion	12
Victoria Papillion	9
Amanda Papillion	8
August Papillion	6
Jimmy Papillion	3

1910 Augusta Papillion

Clementine Gobert Papillion & Augustain Papillion

Frances Papillion LeDee parents

Augustain Papillion and **Clementine Gaubert, Frances'** parents, were married on January 14, 1887 in St. Landry Parish. If calculations are accurate with the year given for his birth (between 1860-1865), **Augustain** would have been about 17-22 years old when he married 15-year-old **Clementine.**

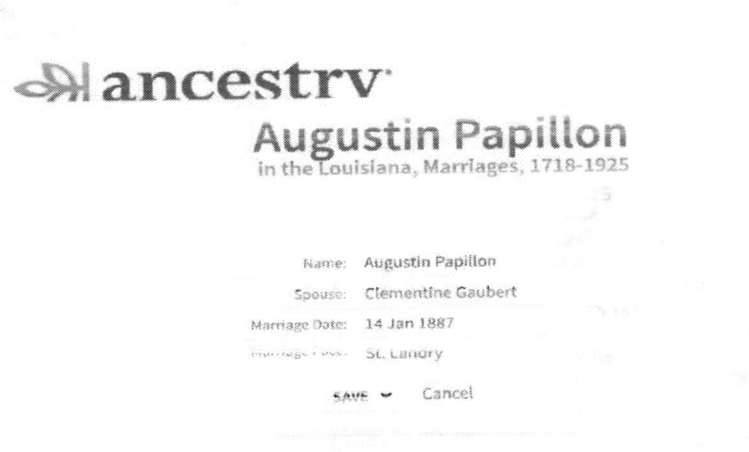
ancestry
Augustin Papillon
in the Louisiana, Marriages, 1718-1925

Name: Augustin Papillon
Spouse: Clementine Gaubert
Marriage Date: 14 Jan 1887
Marriage Place: St. Landry

SAVE Cancel

Find a Grave Memorial for the years 1865 – 1942 provided the burial and cemetery photo of **Auguste Papillion. Nan's** father was about seventy-seven years old at the time of his death.

Auguste Papillion

Birth: Dec. 18, 1865
Death: Feb. 8, 1942

Family links:
Spouse:
Clementine Gobert Papillion (1870 - 1948)*

Children:
Paul Hippolite Papillion (1894 - 1968)*

*Calculated relationship

Burial:
Saint Ann Cemetery
Lawtell
St. Landry Parish
Louisiana, USA

Added by: Jamarick Guillory

Cemetery Photo
Added by: MileHighRob

A census report from the year 1900 was not located for Augustine, and the prior census of 1890 was destroyed at the federal level because of a fire. Therefore, the investigator searched the 1880 census for **Nan's** parents and found her father **Augusta Papillion.** At the time, **Augustain** was a *fifteen-year-old* living with his parents. According to the report, **Augusta** was born in *1865 in the 8th Ward of St. Landry Parish*, Louisiana. He is *mulatto, single*, and *son* to the *head of household.* **Augustain's** parents and paternal grandparents to **Nan** are **Davisson** *age 40,* and **Cilistin** age *42.*

Davisson Papillion has a birthdate of 1840, and his wife **Cilistin** approximately 1838. **Augustain,** at the age of 15 years, is working as a *laborer.* In the family home are **Cedonia** age 18 **(Nan's** paternal aunt), **Colastie** 13, **Leonard** 11, **Adam** age 6, **Polisca** and **Polite Papillion** age 2. It was reported that the average number of children born to a couple during the late 1880's was approximately 8 children.

ancestry

Augusta Papillion

in the 1880 United States Federal Census

Name:	Augusta Papillion
Age:	15
Birth Year:	abt 1865
Birthplace:	Louisiana
Home in 1880:	8th Ward, St Landry, Louisiana
Race:	Mulatto
Relation to Head of House:	Son
Marital Status:	Single
Father's name:	Davisson Papillion
Father's Birthplace:	Louisiana
Mother's name:	Cilistin Papillion
Mother's Birthplace:	Louisiana
Neighbors:	View others on page
Occupation:	Laberor
Cannot read/write:	
Blind:	
Deaf and dumb:	View image
Otherwise disabled:	
Idiotic or insane:	
Household Members:	Name / Age Davisson Papillion / 40

The following is part two of this 1880 census report.

Name	Age
Cilistin Papillion	42
Cedonia Papillion	18
Augusta Papillion	15
Colastie Papillion	13
Leonard Papillion	11
Adam Papillion	6
Polisca Papillion	2
Polite Papillion	2

1880 U.S. Census

Frances' father with his parents and siblings

DUROSSEAU CONNECTION - A SECOND GLANCE

Although this genealogical project has been conducted on **Ozema LeDee,** several years prior to this publication, research was performed on **Lilly Durosseau LeDee's** descendants. While the **Durosseau** material is not as detailed as the **LeDee** information, its disclosure may prove beneficial to numerous individuals.

Lilly's parents were **Jean (John) Baptiste Durosseau** *born in 1872* and **Eva Simien** *born in 1880***.** According to her *Certificate of Baptism* from *St. Anthony of Padua Catholic Church* in Eunice, **Eve Frederic Simien** was the child of **Prien Amie (Joseph Jr.) Simien** who was born in 1845, and **Melanie Provost** who was born in Eunice, Louisiana between the years 1842-1845. It was on *December 22, 1863* that **Joseph Simien** *and* **Melonie Provost** married at *Opelousas Court House.*

Eva Simien Durosseau & Jean Baptiste Durosseau
Parents to Lilly Durosseau LeDee
Circa 1912

Certificate of Baptism

St. Anthony of Padua Catholic Church
P.O. Box 31
Eunice, Louisiana 70535

This is to Certify

That Eve Frederic Simein
Child of Prien Aime' Simein
and Melanie Provat
Born in Eunice, La.
on the 24 day of August 19 1871 was

Baptized

on the 1 day of October 19 1871
according to the
Rite of the Roman Catholic Church
by the Rev. Olivier Bre'
the Sponsors being Joseph Provat, Jr. / Zelisse Louise
as appears from the Baptismal Register of this Church
Dated 2-9-10 Volume 1 Page 36 No. 127
Seal Rev. Gilbert Dutel Pastor
per Deacon [illegible]

On April 26, 1870, the following record from the St. Landry Parish Courthouse described an agreement with clarification of the conveyance made between **Jean Bte Dururseau** and **Pierre Mouille.**

State of Louisiana

We, the undersigned **Pierre Mouille,** and **Jean Bte Durosseau** as principals and **Gertrude Durosseau** _____________and **Antoine Hernandez** as witnesses do hereby certify that the line __________from the cherry tree back of **Mr. Andrepoint's** house, now occupied by the above mentioned **Pierre Mouille** to the part near the fence. Here after that the fence now ___________ be the line. The coffee house still remains in community that the south side belongs to **Mr. Pierre Mouille** and the north side to **Mr. Jean Bte Durosseau**

Eva Simien Durosseau – Lilly Durosseau LeDee's mother

Eva and **Jean Baptiste** were parents to a family of numerous daughters and one son. This listing may/may not include all of their children Pictures have been included for the reader's review. In no specific order, their children were: **Lucy, Melonie, Ana, Lilly, Pierre, Pauline**, and **Alicia. Lilly's** portrait was placed on a previous page in this publication. Also, the author was able to obtain **Pauline's** signature prior to her passing.

Alicia Durosseau

Anna Durosseau

Melonie Durosseau

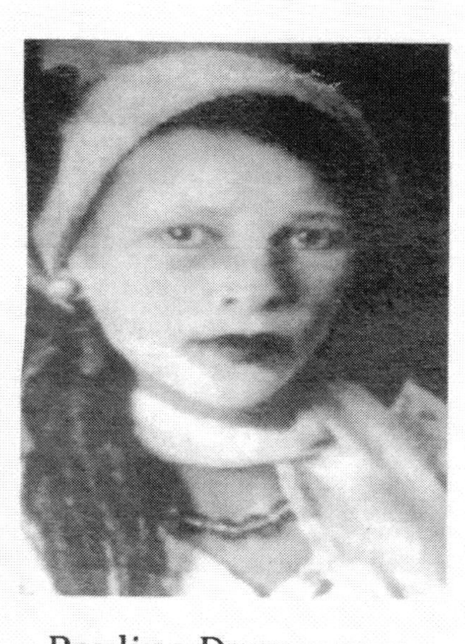

Pauline Durosseau

Pauline durosseau

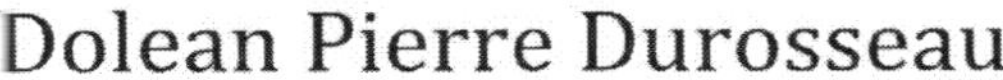

Dolean Pierre Durosseau

Lucy Durosseau

Jean Baptiste Durousseau's parents (**Lilly's** paternal grandparents) were **Jean Baptiste Durosseau** and **Gertrude Ramon.** Reported in the Louisiana census of 1870, **Gertrude** was a native of Mexico. Her birth year is documented as 1821 and she died in 1900 in Louisiana. **Gertrude** and **Jean Baptiste** married March 15, 1839 when the bride was eighteen. Year and place of burial are reported as 1900 in Louisiana. The Spanish influence in the **Durousseau** family came from **Jean Augustin Mateo** from Vera Cruz, Mexico. He married **Anne Marie Guillory,** the sister to **Donato Guillory** and **Evaraste Guillory.** It was their son **Augustin Severin Mateo** who married **Marie Louis Mateo,** the daughter of **Augustin Severin Mateo** and **Marie Josette Ramon.**

Lilly's grandfather **Jean Baptiste Durousseau** who married **Gertrude Ramon** provided the property and materials to build the Catholic Church in Mallet. His name is listed on the cornerstone of the church. There is a road across the prairie from the church which bears the name "**Durousseau Road.**" The property adjacent to this road was once the site of a cotton gin owned by **Jean Baptiste Durousseau.** The

Durousseau family is rich in history with diverse cultural and ethnic backgrounds. According to **Michael John Edwards**, the **Durousseau** family surname originated when two newlyweds went to a pilgrimage in St. Jacgesde Compostellella in Spain in 1538. **Mr. Edwards** additionally stated that, "the first **Durousseau** to America's Southwest region was from Bordeaux, France. **Jean Alexander Cadoin Durosseau** was never issued a land grant but his father-in-law **Donato Bello**, of Corand Naples, Italy, was issued a grant. **Donato Bello** received the land grand for his service in the Spanish military where he achieved the rank of major.

Quebec's Vital and Church Records, the Drouin Collection 1621-1967 is the source of this information.

Until the late 1900s, church registers in Quebec served as civil and vital records in that province. Throughout the years a second copy of church records, from all denominations, was sent annually to the appropriate courthouse. During the 1940s the vital record collections in courthouses throughout Quebec were filmed by the *Institut Généalogique Drouin.* Consequently, this filmed set of records became known as the *Drouin Collection.*

During the enumeration of the census from 1870, **Gertrude** and **Jean Baptiste** were parents to **Adrien, Casimir, Clara, Alice**, and two other household members, **Augustine** and **Joseph.** As head of household, **Jean Baptiste** is a 50-year-old farmer with a substantial share of real and personal estate.

Lilly's paternal great-grandparents were **Jean Alexandre Codoin DuRosseau** *(a cotton planter)* and **Catherine Josette Bello**. **Jean Alexandre Codoin DuRosseau** was reportedly born in 1760 in Bordeaux, France. Located the center of *France's* biggest wine regions, the historic city of *Bordeaux* is also one of the largest in *France*, it offers stunning architecture, a wealth of culture and great varieties of wine. **Catherine (Lilly's** paternal great-grandmother) was the daughter of **Donato Bello**.

While **Donato Bello** was married to **Susanne Mateau,** he and *mulatress* **Marie Jeanne Taillger** *(a free woman of color)* parented **Catherine Donato Bello, Celeste Suzanne Donato Bello,** and **Martin Donato Bello Sr.** During the time, it was common for the wife's children to take the *surname* of her husband, while the children born to his concubine or mistress would accept his *first name* as the surname for his children. Thus, **Donato Bello's** offspring with his wife would be **"Bello"** children. Descendants with his mistress, would carry the surname **"Donato."**

Marie Jeanne Taillger, Catherine's mother, and great-grandmother to **Lilly,** was born around 1746 and died in 1836. **Donato Bello**, her father was born in Naples, Italy in 1732 and died at the age of fifty-five in 1787. Naples, a city in southern Italy, sits on the Bay of Naples. Nearby is Mount Vesuvius, the still-active volcano that destroyed the nearby Roman town Pompeii.

Dating to the 2nd millennium B.C., Naples has centuries of important art and architecture. The city's cathedral, the Duomo di San Gennaro, is filled with frescoes. Two years prior to his death in 1785, **Donato Bello** arrived in Louisiana. He was described as *Italian, 5'6" tall.* According to Southwest Louisiana Records, by **Fr. Hebert**, **Donato Bello** was an *Italian soldier and an officer in the Spanish army.* **Marie Jeanne Taillger/Tailleferr** was a *mulatto* and *free woman of color* from the city of New Orleans The author located no additional information about **Marie.**

Donato Bello's parents were **Victor Bello** (1716-1760) and **Marie de la Maro** (1718). These individuals would be **Lilly Durosseau LeDee's** paternal great-great-grandparents. As resident Italians, **Marie** and **Victor** were married in 1746 at Concord, Archdiocese of Naples, Italy according to Family Search (an online genealogical source.) The **Roman Catholic Archdiocese of Naples or** *Arcidiocesi di Napoli*; is a Roman Catholic Archdiocese in southern Italy. A Christian community was founded there in the 1st century AD and the diocese of Naples was raised to the level of an Archdiocese in the 10th century.

Additionally, **Lilly's** third great grandparents and parents to **Victor Bello,** were **Antonio Bello** (born 1668 in Italy,) and **Aqualima Ramone Lema** (born 1670) in Spain. **Aqualima Ramone Lema** was the daughter of **Jose Timoteo Lema (1630-1697)** and **Ramona Suarez** (1635-1685).

Born before 1734, **Jean Alexandre Codoin's DuRosseau's** parents, and paternal great-great grandparents to **Lilly** were **Jean Simon DuRosseau** and **Marie Vigneras** (who was born before 1738 in Bordeaux, France.)

In 1850, **Eva Simien Durosseau's mother, Melanie Provost** (and maternal grandmother to **Lilly)** was *eight years old* having an estimated *birth year of 1842.*

Melanie listed *Louisiana* as her *birth place* and her *color* as *mulatto.* She is *female,* and residing in *St. Landry Parish, Louisiana.* **Melanie's** parents are identified as **Joleret/Joseph Provost** *age 38* and **Adele Simien Provost** *age 35.* The parents **Joleret** and **Adele Provost** were born between 1812 and 1815 and were maternal grandparents to **Lilly Durosseau LeDee.**

Their granddaughter **Eva/Eve (Mom TEE FEE)** was born on the *24th day of August in 1871* and was baptized on the 1st *day* of *October in 1871.* The reader will notice the discrepancies with the dates provided from census and church records. **Eve's** baptismal sponsors were **Joseph Provost, Jr**, and **Zelisse Louise.**

Although these individuals were born while slavery grew, they were designated Gens de couleur libres or *"free people of color."* What this means for the researcher is that these ancestors could own property and marry without consent. It is also easier to trace their lineage because *free people of color* were listed by name in census documents as well as legal transactions.

Many Creoles of color were free and their descendants often enjoyed many of the same privileges that whites did including property ownership, formal education, and service in the military. While it was not illegal, it was a social taboo for Creoles of color to marry slaves.

According to the Louisiana Death Index, **Madam Joseph Provost** (**Adele**) died in 1873. Yet again, **Adele** was the mother to **Melanie**, grandmother to **Eva Simien Durosseau**. She was about 58 years old at the time of her death. **Melanie's** father **Jobret/Joseph** (maternal great grandparents to **Lilly**) was born in 1812 and was a *cotton planter* by trade.

Lilly, born in 1901, had several other siblings. They were **Anna** born in 1894, **Alicia** in 1897, **Evar** 1899, **Melonie** 1904, **Lucy** 1906, **Dolean Pierre** 1909, and **Pauline** in 1912. Available pictures are provided of **Lilly** and her siblings. Also attached is a picture of **Eva Simien Durosseau** as a young woman. Also included in this section is a baptismal document for **Onie Dourousseau** a child belonging to **Jean Baptiste**

Durosseau and **Eve (Mom TEE FEE) Simien**. **Onie** was born and baptized during the summer of 1894. **Mose Dourousseau** and **Matilde Simien** were the child's baptismal sponsors. **Eva Simien's** parents, **Joseph Simien Jr** born 1845 and her mother **Melanie Provost** born about 1845) were married 22 December 1863. From the 1850 census document, the reader can see the numbers of children that were in the **Melanie Provost** (**Eve Simien Durosseau's aka Mom TEE FEE's** mother) household along with identifying information. Major profession of those in the household was identified as *planters.*

As stated earlier, **Eva's** husband **Jean Baptiste Durosseau** was the son of **Jean Baptiste Durosseau Sr.** and **Gertrude Ramon**. Family discussions reported that **Jean Baptiste** arrived in the United States from his native country; Canada.

A BRIEF BIOGRAPHICAL SKETCH OF OZEMA'S CHILDREN

For the reader's review, here is a brief description of **Zem's** children.

- **Herbert LeDee**
  At the age of 33 **Herbert** passed away of Leukemia. He left behind a wife and five minor children. According to his daughter **Rhonda LeDee**, her father was a devoted family man. Described as submissive and conservative, his final wishes were that his children take care of their mother and their siblings. He also requested that the children attend church each Sunday.

- **Marshall Joseph LeDee**
  According to his daughter **Bridget Isadore,** her dad was playful, supportive, kindhearted and helpful. **Marshall** played a major role in acting as caregiver to his sister, **Leora,** when they were children. Receiving no formal training, he taught himself to play the guitar and became the leading guitarist with the group, **Cookie and the Cupcakes**.

- **John Albert LeDee**
  Known for being kind-hearted, **John** was an avid bowler and past president of Calcasieu Bowling Association. He persevered in his quest when researching his family's history, **John** was a member of Southwest Louisiana Genealogical Society. **John's** profession was as a retired automobile mechanic. Like his two older siblings, **John** died at the age of 63 of cancer.

- **Wilbert (Blackie) LeDee**
  Described as the outgoing, fun-loving, and a playful prankster **Blackie** was the mischief maker of the group. As a youngster, **Blackie** grew up teasing his siblings while being amused at their sometime fearful responses. According to his daughter **Lilly, Blackie** was tremendously creative. As an adult in Lake Charles he operated a paint and body shop and was a successful businessman.

- **Leona LeDee Gallow**
  Zem's oldest daughter, **Leona** is described as sociable, outspoken, and fashion conscious. Younger sister **Leora** stated that she is devoted to her children. She loved attending gatherings and was a great dancer. By profession, **Leona** was a certified nurse at St. Elizabeth's Hospital in Beaumont.

- **Leora Mae LeDee Weiloch**
  A dedicated Licensed Practical Nurse for many years at Illinois Masonic Hospital, **Leora** loved pampering the infants at the facility. Some of her hobbies include bowling, crocheting, playing bingo, fishing and dancing with her father **Zem.** She is thoughtful regarding special occasions. She is sociable, and her daughter **Eartha** stated that she was a strict disciplinarian.

- **Herman Joesin Guillory**
  In the Army Corp. during World War II, **Herman** worked as an aircraft hydraulics' mechanic. His life's work was as an electrician in St. Landry Parish. Prior to his death at age 85, **Herman** suffered from a lengthy illness.

- **Elbert Lee Guillory**
  An opinionated, politically minded, attorney and former state senator, these traits describe **Zem's** son **Elbert Lee**. He is a loyal Republican who is outspoken and unrelenting in his views. During the time of turmoil, and prior to desegregation in the 1960's, **Elbert** was a young civil rights warrior.

- **Lorella LeDee Marshall**
  Educator, member of Delta Sigma Theta Sorority, former member of the Tri-Parish Council Foreign Language Fest, **Lorella** was a training curriculum coordinator for St. Landry Board Bilingual Program. **Lorella** is a dedicated, wife and mother. Prior to her retirement, **Lorella** was heavily involved in social, religious, and academic affairs. She is a sensitive individual and devout Christian.

- **David LeDee**
  Successful businessman and owner of **Dave's Monuments** in Lawtell, **David** has been operating the burial vault business for numerous years. He is always friendly, accommodating, professional, and often involved in civic activities.

- **Willard LeDee**
  A Vietnam veteran and serviceman in the United States Navy, **Willard** is a talented illustrator. As a young man, **Willard** was one of the more creative members of the **LeDee** family. He is a gifted artist whose works have been etched in cooper and leather. He is a deeply religious man who currently lives in California.

- **Jacob LeDee**
  Friendly, caring, pleasant, and a faithful Christian, **"Jake"** is also a Vietnam veteran. He exhibits a somewhat laid-back demeanor, yet he is friendly, easy-going and courteous. He has an immense love of bowling and riding his motorcycle. He is self-assured to win any game of bowling he plays! **Jacob** too has a profession in the burial vault business.

- **Theme John (Tim) LeDee**
  With many years of dedicated work in the area of law enforcement, **Tim** has performed in positions in Crime Prevention, as Officer of the Year, Chief of Detectives, Captain, Sargent, and Lieutenant. He has provided training sessions and seminars to the elderly and spearheaded the development of a program that introduced Drug Awareness Resistance Education to junior high school students.

- **Mose (Moses) LeDee**
  The youngest of the **LeDee** children, **Moses** is described as a reserved family man. He currently works as a mechanic on trains and loves riding his motorcycle.

Vertical (far left) John, Moses, Jacob, Herbert

Bottom row: Leona, David, Elbert Lee, Marshall
Top row: Wilbert (Blackie) Lorella, Tim, Leora, Willard
Insert (top right) Herman

REVISITING THE PAPILLIONS

Because **Zem's** first wife **Lilly** perished tragically in an auto accident, he spent most of his life married to **Frances (Nan) Papillion**. The couple parented six children and were married about 65 years before her death.

While exploring the 1930 census, **Frances,** age about 17 was living in the home with her parents. The document stated that she has *not attended* school and is *unable* *to read or write.* Reported as **Francina Pappallion**, (**Nan)** was *single, Negro,* and daughter to **Augustin Pappallion,** *a 64-year-old male, head of household.* Both of **Nan's** parents were *born in Louisiana* and their home was located *in Police Jury Ward 6 of St. Landry Parish, Louisiana.* A copy of the actual census document is attached for your review.

Others in the household during the census of *1930 include* **Clemontine Pappallion** *60,* **Antlin Pappallion** *20,* **Francinca Pappallion** *17, and* **Willie Pappallion** *age 15.* **Augustin Papillon**, **Frances' (Nan's)** father married his bride **Clementine Gaubert** at St. Landry Parish on January 14, 1887. The source of this information is *Louisiana Marriages 1718-1925.*

During the enumeration of the 1920 Louisiana census, **Francena Papillion** is discovered as an *eight-year-old girl.* It is also revealed that the family is residing in *Police Jury Ward 6* of *St. Landry, Louisiana.* **Francena** is *Mulatto, Female, Daughter,* and *Single.* The report stated that she can *speak English,* has *attended school, and is able to read and write.* Head of household in 1920 is **Ogustain Papillion** *age 55.* Additional family members include **Frances'** mother **Clementine Papillion** *age 51,* **Caror Papillion** *21,* **Amanda Papillion** 17, **Ogust Papillion** 15, **Jammie Papillion** 12, **Anthony Papillion** *10,* **Frances**, then a younger sibling **Willie Papillion** *age 4.*

Ten years earlier in 1910, **Frances**' father **Augusta Papillion** was included in the Louisiana census. There were at least five variations of his name listed. Names reported are **Augusta Papillion, Augustin Peppelion, Augusta Peppelion,** and **Augustas Peppelion.** During this enumeration, **Augustine** is *50 years old* and husband to **Clementine Papillion**, *age 50.* A copy of their portrait is included on page 35.

A cemetery photo is included in this publication for **Auguste Papillion.** The document stated that he was born on *December 18, 1865* and died on *February 8, 1942.* Additionally, **Clementine Gobert Papillion** was *born around 1870,* and passed away in *1948.* Another of the children born to the couple was **Paul Hippolite Papillion** 1894-*1968.*

Others in the home in 1880 were: **Cilistin** age 42 (**Nan's** paternal grandmother), and the couple's children. They were **Cedonia Papillion** 18, **Augusta Papillion** 15, **Colastie Papillion** 13, **Leonard Papillion** 11, **Adam Papillion** 6, **Polisca Papillion** and **Polite Papillion** age 2.

During the twelve years that **Lilly** and **Ozema** were together, they became parents to the six children reported on the previous page. This additional information may prove interesting to the reader as this narrative continues with the ancestors of **Ozema LeDee.**

THE LEDEE' & ROUGEAU ALLIANCE

Known as "**Pop Cause"** by his grandchildren, **Casmier Severin LeDee, Old Dad's** father, was born in February of 1859-1863. For a time, he lived with his son **Zem,** and his granddaughter **Leora** recalls that he was of olive complexion and was not a tall man. According to Louisiana Statewide Death Indices, **Severin Ledet,** *male, Negro, age 82,* **Pop Cause** died on *February 1, 1941.*

According to research, **Pop Cause's** mother **Celestine Rougeau** passed away when her son **Casmier Severin LeDee** was a toddler. His parents were **Augustine LeDee Sr.** (born around 1830) and **Marie Celestine Rougeau** who was born in 1829. The couple married in 1850, and once **Celestine** passed away, **Augustine** married **Marceline Gobert** on May 5, 1870. The following document on page 54 may prove to be fairly accurate yet has not been substantiated.

Augustine LeDee Sr. 1830-1915

ancestry

Celestine Rougeau

BIRTH 8 JAN 1829 • Opelousas, St Landry, Louisiana, United States
DEATH 27 FEB 1866 • Opelousas, St Landry, Louisiana, USA

Facts

Age 0 — **Birth**
8 Jan 1829 • Opelousas, St Landry, Louisiana, United States

Age 1 — **Birth of Sister Genevieve Rougeau** (1830–)
22 Sep 1830 • Louisiana, USA

Age 12 — **Birth of Brother Auguste Rougeau** (1841–)
8 May 1841 • Opelousas, St Landry, Louisiana, United States

Age 13 — **Death of Father Jean Baptiste Rougeau Jr** (1805–1842)
1842 • Opelousas, St Landry, Louisiana, United States

Age 15 — **Birth of Sister Elizabeth Rougeau** (1844–1899)
23 Sep 1844 • Opelousas, St Landry, Louisiana, United States

Age 17 — **Birth of Sister Marie Louise Rougeau** (1846–1912)
22 Sep 1846 • Louisiana, USA

Age 20 — **Birth of Sister Mirza Rougeau** (1849–)
1 Oct 1849 • Opelousas, St Landry, Louisiana, United States

Age 21 — **Marriage**
21 Dec 1850 • Opelousas, St. Landry, Louisiana
Augustin Lede Sr (1830–1915)

Age 21 — **Marriage**
21 Dec 1850 • St. Landry, Louisiana, USA
Augustin Lede Sr (1830–1915)

Age 21 — **Marriage**
21 Dec 1850 • St Landry, Louisiana, USA
Augustin Lede Sr (1830–1915)

Age 21 — **Residence**
1850 • St Landry, Louisiana, USA

Age 22 — **Marriage**
04 Feb 1851 • St. Landry's Ch.(v.A,#52), Opelousas, La.
Augustin Lede Sr (1830–1915)

Age 22 — **Marriage**
04 Feb 1851 • St. Landry's Ch.(v.A,#52), Opelousas, La.
Augustin Lede Sr (1830–1915)

Age 22 — **Birth of Son Augustin Ledee Jr.** (1851–1936)
Nov 1851 • St Landry, Louisiana, USA

Age 23 — **Birth of Daughter Marie Lede** (1853–)
1853 • Louisiana, USA

Family

Parents

Jean Baptiste Rougeau Jr 1805–1842

Celeste Deville 1809–1871

Spouse & Children

Augustin Lede Sr 1830–1915

- **Augustin Ledee Jr.** 1851–1936
- **Marie Lede** 1853–
- **Celeste Lede** 1853–1929
- **Louis Lede** 1854–1941
- **Loni Lede** 1856–
- **Victoire Lede** 1856–
- **Sydonie Lede** 1858–
- **Alicia Olivia Lede** 1861–1948
- **Simeon Lede** 1863–1885
- **Severin Sept Casmir Lede Sr** 1863–1941
- **Eve Lede** 1874–1923
- **Felicite Lede** 1875–1876
- **Adam Lede** 1879–1926
- **Jean Baptiste Ceran (John) Lede** 1881–
- **Marie Odilia Lede** 1886–1902

For clarification, **Ol Dad's** paternal grandparents (parents to **Severan Casmier LeDee)** were **Celestine** and **Augustine LeDee Sr**. The previous page shows a picture of the **Augustine (Ol Dad's** grandfather.)

Because his wife **Celestine** had passed before his children were grown, **Augustine** filed this transcribed document with the court. It stated:

To the Honorable, the Judge of the 8th Judicial District of the state of Louisiana holding session in and for the parish of St. Landry.

The petition of **Augustin Lede**, with respect represents that his wife **Celestine Rougot,** free woman of color lately died in the parish leaving eight minor children issue of his legal marriage. With said deceased to wit, **Augustin Celestine, Louis, Victorire, Sedonia, Cazimire, Alicia,** and **Simon Le'De**, your petitioner further a??? that he has qualified as natural tutor of his said minors and that he has caused an under tutor to be appointed to said minors. Petitioner prayers that an under ___ may issue authorizing **Yves Pavy** Recorder of said parish to call and to hold a family meeting of said minors of **?rail Rougot, Donate Guillory, Evariste Guillory** and **Caziimere Guillory** nearest relatives to said minors for the purposes of advising on the best move of disposing of the property held in community said heirs and your petitioners......

To the Hble The judge of the 8th
judicial Dist of the state of Louisiana
holding session in and for the
Parish of St Landry

The petition of Augustin Lede
With respect represents
That his wife Celestine Rougot
f w of collor lattly Died in this
parish leaving eight minor chil-
dren issue of his legal marriage
With said Decd to wit Augustin,
Celestine, Louis, Victoire, Sedonia,
Cazimire, Alicia and Simon Ledé
your petitioner further avers
That he has qualified as natural
Tutor of his said minors and
That he has caused an Under
Tutor to be appointed to
said minors
Petitioner prays that an
order may issue authorising
Yves Pavy Recorder of said parish
to call and to hold a family
meeting of said minors composed of Frail Rougot,
Saint Clair Rougot, Donate Guillory
Evarist Guillory and Cazimire Guillory
nearest relation of said minors,
for the purpose of advising
on the best move of disposing of the property

ancestry

Celestine Rougeau

BIRTH 8 JAN 1829 • Opelousas, St Landry, Louisiana, United States
DEATH 27 FEB 1866 • Opelousas, St Landry, Louisiana, USA

Facts

Age 0 — **Birth**
8 Jan 1829 • Opelousas, St Landry, Louisiana, United States

Age 1 — **Birth of Sister Genevieve Rougeau** (1830–)
22 Sep 1830 • Louisiana, USA

Age 12 — **Birth of Brother Auguste Rougeau** (1841–)
8 May 1841 • Opelousas, St Landry, Louisiana, United States

Age 13 — **Death of Father Jean Baptiste Rougeau Jr** (1805–1842)
1842 • Opelousas, St Landry, Louisiana, United States

Age 15 — **Birth of Sister Elizabeth Rougeau** (1844–1899)
23 Sep 1844 • Opelousas, St Landry, Louisiana, United States

Age 17 — **Birth of Sister Marie Louise Rougeau** (1846–1912)
22 Sep 1846 • Louisiana, USA

Age 20 — **Birth of Sister Mirza Rougeau** (1849–)
1 Oct 1849 • Opelousas, St Landry, Louisiana, United States

Age 21 — **Marriage**
21 Dec 1850 • Opelousas, St. Landry, Louisiana
Augustin Lede Sr (1830–1915)

Age 21 — **Marriage**
21 Dec 1850 • St. Landry, Louisiana, USA
Augustin Lede Sr (1830–1915)

Age 21 — **Marriage**
21 Dec 1850 • St Landry, Louisiana, USA
Augustin Lede Sr (1830–1915)

Age 21 — **Residence**
1850 • St Landry, Louisiana, USA

Age 22 — **Marriage**
04 Feb 1851 • St. Landry's Ch.(v.A,#52), Opelousas, La.
Augustin Lede Sr (1830–1915)

Age 22 — **Marriage**
04 Feb 1851 • St. Landry's Ch.(v.A,#52), Opelousas, La.
Augustin Lede Sr (1830–1915)

Age 22 — **Birth of Son Augustin Ledee Jr.** (1851–1936)
Nov 1851 • St Landry, Louisiana, USA

Age 23 — **Birth of Daughter Marie Lede** (1853–)
1853 • Louisiana, USA

Family

Parents

- **Jean Baptiste Rougeau Jr** 1805–1842
- **Celeste Deville** 1809–1871

Spouse & Children

- **Augustin Lede Sr** 1830–1915
  - **Augustin Ledee Jr.** 1851–1936
  - **Marie Lede** 1853–
  - **Celeste Lede** 1853–1929
  - **Louis Lede** 1854–1941
  - **Loni Lede** 1856–
  - **Victoire Lede** 1856–
  - **Sydonie Lede** 1858–
  - **Alicia Olivia Lede** 1861–1948
  - **Simeon Lede** 1863–1885
  - **Severin Sept Casmir Lede Sr** 1863–1941
  - **Eve Lede** 1874–1923
  - **Felicite Lede** 1875–1876
  - **Adam Lede** 1879–1926
  - **Jean Baptiste Ceran (John) Lede** 1881–
  - **Marie Odilia Lede** 1886–1902

Sources

Ancestry Sources

After his wife **Celestine's** passing, **Augustine** married **Marceline Gobert** on May 30, 1870. During the census of 1910, **Augustan Lada** was *82 years old,* having an estimated birthyear of *1828.* The census stated that he was residing in Mallet in 1910, is *mulatto, male, head of household,* and *married* to **Marceline Lada**. *French* is the *family's native tongue,* and **Augustine** is working as a *farmer.* The family home is *owned free; not mortgaged.*

During the enumeration of the 1930 census, **Severin LeDe (Zem's** father) is married and residing on an *unimproved district* of St. Landry Parish. Living on a *farm,* the family is *renting* their home, and *do not own a radio set.* **Severin** reports that he has *not attended school* but is *able to read and write.* As *head of household,* he has an occupation of *farmer,* and works on a *general farm.* Both of **Severin's** parents were purportedly *born in Louisiana.* During this 1930 enumeration, **Henry** their 17-year-old grandson is living with **Severin** and **Marie Teresa**. As grandparents they are described as *ages 70* and *66 years* respectively.

The next image is a portrait of **Mom TAA Ya**, the mother of **Ozema LeDee** and wife to **Casmier Severin LeDee.** The picture is poor in quality, yet the only one available at the time of this writing.

The following document is a summary of facts from Ancestry. The details of this report are unsupported by the researcher.

According to the Bureau of Vital Statistics, **Ol' Dad's** father **Severin Ledet** lived his entire life in Mallet, LA. He died at the approximate *age of 82 years old* on February 2, 1941. His son **Ozema** signed as informant on his death certificate. **Severin's** date of birth was given as *February 1859.* **Severin's** certificate of death reports that he died of cerebral thrombosis, or a blood clot in the brain. Furthermore, the document stated that he was senile, which was due to psychosis; a severe mental disorder in which thought, and emotions are so impaired that contact is lost with external reality. Senility is a severe mental deterioration in old age, characterized by loss of memory and sometimes control of bodily functions. Family members once reported that **Severin** lived with his son **Ozema,** (and his family), where he may have been restrained to prevent him from wandering or injuring himself.

DEPARTMENT OF COMMERCE
Bureau of the Census
District No. 49-5481A

STATE OF LOUISIANA
BUREAU OF VITAL STATISTICS
CERTIFICATE OF DEATH

State File No. 2867
Registrar's No. 1349

1. PLACE OF DEATH: (a) Parish St. Landry Ward 6 (b) City or town Rural

2. USUAL RESIDENCE OF DECEASED: (a) State La. (b) Parish St. Landry (c) City or town Rural (d) Street No. Opelousas La. Rt. 4

3(a) FULL NAME Severin Sedet Sr

4. Sex M 5. Color or race Col 6(a) Single, widowed, married, divorced Married

7. Birth date of deceased Feb. 1859

8. AGE: 82 (8) (11)

MEDICAL CERTIFICATION

20. Date of death: Month 2 day 1 year 1941

Immediate cause of death Cerebral thrombosis; generalized arteriosclerosis; senile ... Due to psychosis

Of autopsy None

18(a) Signature of funeral director ... (b) Address Opelousas

19(a) 2-5-41 (Date received local registrar) (Registrar's signature)

MARGIN RESERVED FOR BINDING

N. B.—WRITE PLAINLY WITH UNFADING INK—THIS IS A PERMANENT RECORD. Every item of information should be carefully supplied. AGE should be stated EXACTLY. PHYSICIANS should state CAUSE OF DEATH in plain terms, so that it may be properly classified. Exact statement of OCCUPATION is very important.

ancestry

Severin Casmir Lede

BIRTH 1859 • Louisiana
DEATH 1 FEB 1941 • St. Landry, Louisiana, USA

Facts

Age 0 — **Birth**
1859 • Louisiana

Age 7 — **Death of Mother Celestine Rougeau** (1829–1866)
27 Feb 1866 • Opelousas, St Landry, Louisiana, United States

Age 11 — **Residence**
1870 • Ward 5, St Landry, Louisiana, USA
Post Office: Bayou Chicot

Age 22 — **Marriage**
1881
Theresia Ledee (1867–1945)

Age 23 — **Birth of Son Sev* L*Li** (1882–)
Oct 1882 • Louisiana

Age 23 — **Birth of Son Severin Ledee** (1882–1966)
19 Oct 1882 • Louisiana

Age 25 — **Birth of Daughter Lydia M L*Li** (1884–)
Oct 1884 • Louisiana

Age 25 — **Birth of Daughter Lydia W. Ledee** (1884–)
Oct 1884 • Louisiana

Age 25 — **Birth of Daughter Marie Theresia LEDE** (1884–)
19 OCT 1884 • Opelousas Louisiana

Age 28 — **Birth of Son Victoran Lada** (1887–1975)
10 Mar 1887 • Mallet, St. Landry, Louisiana

Age 29 — **Marriage**
13 Jan 1888 • St. Landry, Louisiana, USA
Theresia Ledee (1867–1945)

Age 29 — **Birth of Son Victorin L*Li** (1888–)
Mar 1888 • Louisiana

Age 31 — **Birth of Son Victor Leday** (1890–1918)
30 Jul 1890 • Eunice, Louisiana

Age 32 — **Birth of Son Victor Lada** (1892–1918)
abt 1892 • Louisiana

Age 33 — **Birth of Son Augustin Ledee** (1892–)
18 Oct 1892 • Louisiana

Age 34 — **Birth of Daughter Evelin L*Li** (1893–)
Jul 1893 • Louisiana

Family

Parents

Augustin Lede 1830–1915

Celestine Rougeau 1829–1866

Spouse & Children

Theresia Ledee 1867–1945

- **Augustin Lede** 1829–
- **Sev* L*Li** 1882–
- **Severin Ledee** 1882–1966
- **Lydia M L*Li** 1884–
- **Lydia W. Ledee** 1884–
- **Marie Theresia LEDE** 1884–
- **Victoran Lada** 1887–1975
- **Victorin L*Li** 1888–
- **Victor Leday** 1890–1918
- **Victor Lada** 1892–1918
- **Augustin Ledee** 1892–
- **Evelin L*Li** 1893–
- **Alvia Lada** 1895–
- **Frank L*Li** 1895–
- **Frank Ledee** 1898–
- **Amelia L*Li** 1900–
- **Orelia Lada** 1900–1979
- **Ozene Ledee** 1903–2005
- **Ogama Lada** 1904–

Age 36 — **Birth of Daughter Alvia Lada** (1895–)
abt 1895 • Louisiana

Age 36 — **Birth of Son Frank L*Li** (1895–)
Aug 1895 • Louisiana

Age 39 — **Birth of Son Frank Ledee** (1898–)
abt 1898 • Louisiana

Age 40 — **Birth of Daughter Orelia Lada** (1900–1979)
abt 1900 • Louisiana

Age 40 — **Birth of Daughter Amelia L*Li** (1900–)
Jan 1900 • Louisiana

Age 41 — **Residence**
1900 • Police Jury Ward 8, Saint Landry, Louisiana, USA
Marital Status: Married; Relation to Head of House: Head

Age 44 — **Birth of Son Ozene Ledee** (1903–2005)
02-26-1903 • Mallet, Louisiana

Age 44 — **Birth of Son Ogama Lada** (1904–)
abt 1904 • Louisiana

Age 45 — **Birth of Son Freddie LEDE** (1904–1956)
10 Jul 1904 • St. Landry, Louisiana

Age 45 — **Birth of Son Yves LEDE** (1905–1926)
19 Jun 1905 • Opelousas, St.Landry, Louisiana

Age 47 — **Birth of Son Eive Lada** (1907–)
abt 1907 • Louisiana

Age 51 — **Residence**
1910 • Mallet, Saint Landry, Louisiana, USA
Marital Status: Married; Relation to Head of House: Head

Age 54 — **Birth of Son henry Ledee** (1913–2006)
20 Feb 1913 • Louisiana, United States

Age 56 — **Death of Father Augustin Lede** (1830–1915)
04 Sep 1915 • St Landry, Louisiana, USA

Age 59 — **Death of Son Victor Leday** (1890–1918)
24 Oct 1918 • Louisiana

Age 59 — **Death of Son Victor Lada** (1892–1918)
24 Oct 1918 • Louisiana

Age 67 — **Death of Son Yves LEDE** (1905–1926)
2 Nov 1926 • Louisiana

Age 70 — **Death of Sister Celeste Lede** (1853–1929)
09 Jan 1929 • St Landry, Louisiana, USA

Age 71 — **Residence**
1930 • Police Jury Ward 6, St Landry, Louisiana
Marital Status: Married; Relation to Head of House: Head

Age 77 — **Death of Brother Augustin LeDe Jr.** (1851–1936)
19 Dec 1936 • ,,Louisiana

Death of Brother Louis Lede (1854–1941)
1941

Freddie LEDE 1904–1956

Yves LEDE 1905–1926

Eive Lada 1907–

henry Ledee 1913–2006

Sources

Ancestry Sources

1870 United States Federal Census

1900 United States Federal Census

1910 United States Federal Census

1930 United States Federal Census

Ancestry Family Trees

Louisiana Statewide Death Index, 1900-1949

Louisiana, Marriages, 1718-1925

U.S., Social Security Applications and Claims Index, 1936-2007

Here are a few photographs of **Zem's** siblings. From left to right are **Marie Evelin, Frank,** and below them are pictured**, Victor,** and **Victortorian.** From Ancestry, there appears to have been at least eleven children born to **Severin Casmir LeDee** and **Marie Theresa Richard.**

An examination of the 1920 and 1910 census reports for Several and Marie Teresa, generated no results, consequently the author therefore examined the available 1900 document. During this 1900 enumeration, the family home is *owned* and *not mortgaged.* Seven children are in the home ranging in ages of *4 months* to *age 17.*

Severin Lede/Severin Lede Sr. Sev*N Lede Jr, Ssionn Leeli all describe **Ozema LeDee's** father. **Severin (Pop Cause**) is 37 years old in 1900 with a birth date of February 1863. He is described as living in Police Jury Ward 8 in Saint Landry Parish, Louisiana. He is *male, black, head of household, married in 1881.* **Old Dad's** parents, **Severin** and **Marie Teresa** have been married for *nineteen years,* with 1881 as the specific year. The census document stated that **Marie Teresa** had given birth to nine children at the time of this enumeration; seven of the nine had survived. (**Mom TAA Ya) Marie Teresa Richard LeDee** was born in 1866 and passed away in 1945.

While two of **Zem's** children **Leona** and **Leora,** were outside playing, (in 1945) twelve-year-old **Leora** believed what she saw was a vision of her grandmother, **Mom TAA Ya.** Immediately the girls ran home to announce to **Nan** what was witnessed and reported that their grandmother had just died. **Nan** told them "Don't say that cher!" Within a short time, someone drove to the family home and delivered the news that **Mom TAA Ya** had indeed passed away.

Marie Teresa Richard LeDe's death record from Louisiana State Archives stated, that at the time of her death, she was an *81-year-old widow* from *Mallet.* The keeping of *vital records* did not become a statewide mandate in *Louisiana* until 1914. The recording of vital events prior to this year was sometimes inconsistent. During her productive years **Zem's** mother, **Mom TAA Ya** once farmed in rural Mallet. **Mom TAA Ya's** previous residence was in the community of Pot Cove. **Zem's** maternal grandparents were **R. Richard**, and **Sophie Richard** according to her death certificate. **Marie Teresa Richard's** death was due to *cerebral hemorrhage* (stroke) caused by *five years of hypertension* (high blood pressure.)

Casmier's mother, **Celestine Rougeau** passed away when he (**Pop Cause**) was approximately three years old. The Civil War, fighting between the states, was in progress for another couple of years before its ending in 1865. **Casmier Severin** father was **Augustine LeDe Sr.** The *Civil War* of 1861-1865 determined what kind of nation we would be. The war resolved two fundamental questions; whether the United States was to be a Northern victory in the war and preserved the United States as one nation thereby ending the institution of slavery. The Civil War came at the cost of 625,000 lives-nearly as many American soldiers as died in all the other wars in which this country has fought combined. The American Civil War was the largest and most destructive conflict in the Western world. **Zem's** father **Casmier** was born during this Civil War era.

As reported in Ancestry, **Pop Cause** and his wife **Marie Teresa Richard** parented the following children: **Severin Jr., Lydia, Victorin, Evelin, Frank, Orelia, Ozene, Ogama**, and **Ewe. Marie Teresa Richard** and **Severin LeDe** were married on January 13, 1888 in St. Landry Parish.

OZEMA'S PATERNAL GRANDPARENTS

As we proceed to an earlier generation, the parents of **Casmier Severin Lede** and grandparents to **Ozema** are revealed. This third-generation ancestry of **Zem** was **Pop Cause's** father, **Augustine LeDe Sr**. He was born in Louisiana in 1830 and passed away in 1915 at the age of 85. *A Found A Grave Memorial* is included in this chronicle and states that **Augustine** is buried at Saint Ann Cemetery in Lawtell.

When the 1910 census was enumerated, **Augustine** was reportedly *82 years old, married, living in Mallet, male, head of household*, native tongue is *French*, occupation is *farmer*, and he *owns his home* which is a *farm*. His spouse is listed as **Marceline Lada.** The document additionally stated that he *has not* attended school and is *unable to read* or *write.*

Augustine was approximately 34 years old when **Pop Cause** was born. He was first married to **Marie Celestine Rougeau** in 1850. **Marie Celestine** was born in 1829. As stated earlier, her son **Casmier Severin** was a toddler when his mother passed away according to Ancestry.

The following document was located at the St. Landry Parish Courthouse outlining the following information that is transcribed here.

Casmier Severin's mother, **Celestine Rougeau** has a birth date of January 8, 1829 and her death was recorded as February 27, 1866. At the time of her death, she was about 37 years old. **Celestine's** parents were reported as **Jean Baptiste Rougeau** and **Celeste Deville.**

It was reported in *Louisiana Compiled Marriage Index 1718-1925,* that **Augustin Lede** married his new bride **Marceline Gobert** on May 30, 1870 in St. Landry Parish.

As reported by the 1860 census, all reported here were *free persons of color.* The year this census was taken, Augustine is 31 having an approximate birth year of 1829. **Augustin** was born in the *state of Louisiana* and the *town of Mallet.* He is reported as *Mulatto, Head of household,* and *married* for *23 years. Occupation* is revealed as *farmer* and the family's *native tongue is French.* The census additionally stated that **Augustin** *is the* father to *nine children* and *has never attended school.* He is *incapable* of *writing and/or reading.* The family's *farm* is *no longer mortgaged.*

An investigation of the 1850 Louisiana census reveals that **Celestine Rougeau** is *nineteen* years old, *female, mulatto,* with a *birth year* of *1831*. Therefore, the reader can surmise that there is a discrepancy of 2-3 years regarding her year of birth. Her mother **Celestine** is 50 years old, and her father is reported as **Casimer Rougeau** age 54. Perhaps her son **Pop Cause (Casmier)**, **Zem's** father was named after his grandfather.

The following information from *Ancestry* has not been confirmed, but states that **Augustine** was 20 years old when he married **Marie Celestine Rougeau** on December 21, 1850 in St. Landry Parish.

Their courthouse document recorded the following information regarding the marriage of **Augustine** and **Celeste**. A copy of the actual handwritten document is attached.

> State of Louisiana
> Parish of St. Landry
>
> Know all men by these present that **Augustin LeDe'** as principal and **Casimier Roujeau** as security both of the State of Louisiana and parish of St. Landry are held and firmly bound unto **Joseph Walker,** Governor of the State of Louisiana and his successors in office in the sum of three hundred dollars which sum will ___?_____ truly to be paid, they find themselves, their heirs executors and administrators jointly and severely:
>
> In testimony whereof they have hereto signed at Opelousas these 21st day of December A.D. 1850.
> The condition of the above obligation is such that whereas the above **Augustin LeDe'** has this day obtained license to marry **Miss Celeste Rougeau** also of said Parish. Now if there should here after appeared no legal impediment to said marriage then and in that case the said obligation to be null and void.

Together the couple parented **Augustine LeDe Jr**. in 1851, **Marie** in 1852, **Celeste** in 1853, **Louis** in 1854, **Victoire** in 1856, and **Sydonie** in 1858, **Alicia Olivia** in 1861, **Severin** in 1862, **Simeon** in 1863, and **Louis** in 1865 Others later discovered were: **Eve** in 1874, **Felicite** in 1875, **Adam** in 1879, **Jean Baptiste Ceran** in 1881 and **Marie Odilia** in 1886. It must be remembered that birth certificates were not required until many years later.

As reported in *Louisiana Marriages 1718-1925*, **Augustin LeDe** and **Marceline Gobert** married in *St. Landry Parish* on *May 30, 1870.* With his second wife **Marceline Gobert, Augustine** fathered **Mentine** in 1871, **Eave** in 1878, and **Adon** in 1879. During the enumeration of the 1870 census, **Augustine Ledais** is a *farmer* and his wife **Marcelin** is *keeping house.* At this time, there are eight children under their care, ages seven through nineteen.

There were a great number of conveyances at the St. Landry Parish Courthouse regarding **Ozema LeDee's** paternal grandfather, **Augustine.** From the legal document of 1859 **Augustin Lede'** free man of color vs **Julien Guillory** free man of color regarding an appeal from the Justice of the Peace states:

> Know all men by their present that **Julien Guillory** free man of color as principal and **Emanuel Guillory** as Security are held and firmly bound unto **Augustin LeDe'** free man of color into the sum of Eighty three dollars for which payment will and truly to be made to the said **Augustin Lede'** f.m.c. and to his heirs, executors and administrators and assigns, we do bound ourselves ____________?________ severely, our heirs, executors, and administrators firmly by their presents; signed with our hands and sealed with our seals, at the Parish of St. Landry this day October 1859.
>
> Whereas, the above bound principal, **Julian Guillory** f.m.c. has this day taken an appeal from a certain judgement rendered against him by the undersigned Justice of the Peace acting in and for the parish of St. Landry in favor of the said **Augustin Lede'** for the sum of Seventy-two dollars which judgement is numbered on the docket of said Justice as N. 118.
>
> Now, therefore, the condition of the above obligation is such that of the said bound principal **Julien Guillory** shall pay such sum as shall be awarded against him in the said appeal, then, and in such case the above obligation to be null and void, otherwise to remain in full force and virtue.
>
> Signed sealed, and acknowledged in presence of us this 14th day of October 1859
>
> Before me: Joseph Chenier Justice of the Peace St. Landry

OZEMA'S LINEAGE CONTINUED

Paternal grandfather to **Casmier Severin LeDee (Pop Cause)** was **Antoine Valenten LeDe'** whose birth year is recorded as 1805. This individual is paternal great grandfather to **Zem. Antoine**, father to **Augustin LeDe'** lived to the age of 63 years. Three marriage documents were located at the St. Landry Parish Courthouse for **Antoine**. The initial filing for a marriage occurred February 15, 1831 to **Louise Simien.** By 1860, there was an **Antoine LeDe'** who married **Olivia George Simien.** Then by 1863, there was an **Antoine LeDe'** who wedded **Celestine/Genevieve Celest George Simien** in 1863. It was problematic to determine if these **Antoine LeDe'** men were the same individuals.

Stated in one document was that **Antoine Valentine LeDee** married **Honorine Mateo** and the couple parented **Sidonie LeDee** in 1823 when he was eighteen years old. He later became father to **Augustine LeDe Sr.** in 1830 when he was twenty-five years old. **Marie Louise LeDee** and **Antone Valentine LeDee** were children with his wife **Marie Louise Simien.** This information was submitted to Ancestry and has not been substantiated by the writer of this publication.

Some of the wealthier and prosperous Creoles of color owned slaves themselves. Such ownership was often used to support their social position and fund the abolitionist cause. At the enumeration of the 1840 census, **Valentin LeDe'** was approximately thirty-five years old. Earlier enumerations did not provide specific information regarding occupation, education, or names of household members. Thus, **Valentin LeDe,** head of household at his home in St. Landry Parish had the following individuals in his home:

Free Colored Persons – Males – Under the age of ten = 2
Free Colored Persons – Males – Whose ages are between 24 - 35 = 1
Free Colored Persons – Females – Under the age of ten = 2
Free Colored Persons – Females - Whose ages are between 10-23 = 1
Free Colored Persons - Females - Whose ages are between 24-35 = 1
Slaves – Females - Whose ages are between 10-23 = 1
Total Free Colored Persons = 7
Total Slaves = 1
Total All Persons – Free White, Free Colored, and Slaves = 8

Filed by the court on January 26, 1887 regarding the death of Antoine Ledet the following information was obtained:

To the Honorable George W. _______ Judge of 13th Judicial District Court for St. Landry Parish

The petition of **Celestine Simien**, a resident of St. Landry Parish, with respect represents That her husband **Antoine Ledet,** died in said parish about two years ago leaving seven minor children ______of his marriage with petitioner the names of said minors are **Filias, Genvine, Mare Louise, Alexandrina, Antoinette, Leonce,** and **Bridget.**
Her said husband left also some moveable property. Petitioner represents that she is in __dreadful_ circumstances owing very little property in her own right, the same being worth but more than four hundred dollars.
Petitioner represents further that **Jules Perrodine** of St Landry Parish has signed and attached some property belonging to the estate of her said deceased husband and upon which your petitioner in her capacity of natural tutrix has by operations of law a privilege granted in such cases to her for her minor children in alarming circumstances.
Petitioner desires to qualify as natural tutrix to her said minors. Then an inventory should be taken of the property of her said deceased husband as the ________?_______.

A year prior to the above filing, **Valentin Ledet** (an older son of the deceased Antoine Valentin) represents that he will act as under tutor (guardian) to the minor children of **Antoine Valentin Ledet** (his father.)

The legal document stated:

THE STATE OF LOUISIANA
PARISH OF ST. LANDRY

I **Valentin Ledet,** of the State of Louisiana and Parish of St. Landry, do solemnly swear that I will and faithfully perform all and singular, the duties and functions incumbent on me as Under tutor to **Filias, Genvieve, Marie Louise, Alesandrina, Antoinette, Leonce, and Bridget,** minor issue of the marriage of **Celestine Simien** with **Antoine Ledet** deceased.
To the best of my judgement and abilities, according to law---So help me God.
Sworn to and Subscribed at Opelousas this 27th day of December 1886.

A second article related to the previous courthouse document stated:

THE STATE OF LOUISIANA)
PARISH OF ST. LANDRY)

To all whom it may concern:

Be it known that I **Benjamin F.** _____________Deputy Clerk of the Thirteenth District Court in and for the aforesaid parish have this day, the 27th of December in year one thousand eight hundred and eight six, by virtue of an order of the Honorable G W. Hudspeth, Judge of said District Court bearing date the 22nd day of December 1886 appointed and do hereby appoint **Valentine Ledet** under tutor to **Filias, Genevieve, Marie Louise, Alexandriana, Antoinette, Leonce,** and **Bridget,** minor issue of the marriage of Celestine Simien with Antoine Ledet deceased hereby vesting him the said **Valentine Ledet** as under tutor with all the powers and authorities contemplated by the laws of this State in such cases made and provided the previous requisites of the law having been complied with.

In testimony whereof, I have hereunto signed and affixed the seal of my office at Opelousas the day and year above written.

For your review, a duplicate of the authentic document is attached. Additional legal proceedings regarding the above matter continued as the following document reports:

State of Louisiana
Parish of St. Landry
We, the undersigned members of family meeting of the minor issue of the marriage of **Antoine Lede** deceased with **Celestine Simien** surviving widow, solemnly and s_________ answer that we will give our advice touching the interest of said minors in relation to a partition of two tracts of land bound in common between said minors and the major heirs of **Marie Louise Simien** deceased, wife of **Valentin Lede Sr**. both deceased to the list of our ability and understanding. So help us God.
sworn to be subscribed before me
This 23th day November 1889.

Subsequent to the above reported document, the following court proceeding took place. Because much of the document is illegible, the author ask that the reader use his/her own personal interpretation.

To the Honorable Judge of the 13th Judicial District of La in and for the Parish of St. Landry.

The petition of **Celestine Simien,** widow of **Antoine Lede'** deceased, and natural tutrix (guardian) to her minor children, the issue of her marriage to the said **Antoine Lede'.** With respect represent that a family meeting of her minor children viz, **Geneive, Marie Louise, Alexandrine, Antoinette, Leonce**, and **Bridget Lede'** that said meeting was conducted for the purposes of advising and touching the interest of said minors in _____?____ with their co heirs, the heirs of **Marie Louise Lede'** widow **Valentin Lede Sr.** That said meeting was held today before **J. L. Chachere**, Notary Public. That they here decided that the land should be sold for cash and here appraised the same at three dollars per arpent (a measure of slightly less than an acre) and have authorized **Celestine Simien**, widow **Antoine Lede'** natural tutrix of said minors to sell the same for cash for no less than the appraised value.

Where for the premises considered petitioner prays that the providing of said family meeting be ho?______ and confirmed and she prays for all other orders be _______?______ for final relief.

Although **Victorien LeDee** may not have been a direct ancestor to **Ozema,** (he was **Zem's** great-great uncle) the following document proved to be fascinating and thought-provoking. It has been transcribed for ease in reading. The contract transpired and was documented in 1818.

This indenture made this seventeenth day of December, in the Year of our Lord, one thousand eight hundred and eighteen.

With forth, that for __?__ good causes and consideration **Victorien LeDee** a free boy of colour aged seventeen years, by and with the consent of his father **Paul LeDe**; hath bound and put himself apprentice unto **Jose Diaz** to learn the art, trade, mystery of occupation of shoemaking which the said **Jose Diaz** now useth and to dwell and continue with the said **Jose Diaz** his executors of administration from the day of the date herefor until the full and term of two years-during all which periods said apprentice shall faithfully serve his master and obey his orders and lawful commands and not depart said service without his consent of the said master. The apprentice in the said art, trade, mystery of occupation aforesaid with all things thereunto belonging shall and wilt teach of cause to be taught and shall during the would of said period find said apprentice with good and sufficient food, meat, drink, washing, lodging and apparel.
For witnesses whereof the said **Victorien Lede** hath hereto set his mark not knowing how to write at the Parish of Saint Landry the day and year first above written.—signed, sealed, and delivered in presence of **George King**, Judge in and for the Parish of Saint Landry of **Paul Lede'** father of said apprentice and of **Guy H. Bell** and **Luke Lefafsier** subscribing witnesses **Victorien** (his ordinary mark) **LeDe, Paul LeDe** and **Jose Diaz.**

The **Paul LeDe'** referred to in the previous document is the father of **Antoine Valentin LeDe'. Paul** and his wife **Marie Ann Grenier Laviolette,** born 1762**,** were **Antoine's** parents, and paternal great-great grandparents to **Ozema LeDee. Paul** has a birth year between 1735-1737 and died in 1823. meaning that he lived well into his eighties. It was reported that **Paul** was born in Opelousas and died in St. Landry Parish. He and **Maria Ann Grenier Laviolette** (born in 1780) married in 1794 in the United States. According to Family Search, the **Laviolette** families were from Saint, Ours, sur, Richelieu, Rouville, Quebec, Canada. There was no indication regarding the names of **Paul LeDe's** parents. Also, there is no indication as to when **Marie Ann** died.

One report through Ancestry stated that **Marianne Laviolette** parented a son in 1793 at the age of 13 years old. It was in Quebec where **Marie Anne** was baptized. She then married at age 14 in 1794 and had a second son in 1795. By the time she was twenty-five in 1805, she gave birth to **Antoine Valentine Ledee**, a direct progenitor to **Ozema LeDee.** Information through Ancestry outlining this report is attached.

When **Marie Ann** was about 21 years old, her father **Francois Grenier** died in 1801; he was seventy-one years old. **Marie Ann's** mother is reported as **Angelique Choret** who was born in 1730; she passed away on April 5, 1807.

OZEMA'S THIRD GREAT GRANDPARENTS

This publication began with our ancestors residing in the United States. By the year 1730, the search continues in Canada. **Angelique Choret,** and **Charles Francois Grenier** were parents to **Marie Ann**. These individuals are then the direct paternal (third) great-great-great grandparents to **Ozema LeDee. Angelique** was born April 26, 1730 in Saint Antoine de Tilly, Quebec, Canada. By the time she was nineteen in 1750, she married **Francois Grenier**. The couple's marriage took place in Ste Croix, Lotbiniere, Quebec, Canada. With Ancestry as a source of this information the reader can see from the following document that **Angelique** had more than twelve children.

Charles Francois Grenier, husband to **Angelique Choret** from the previous two passages, was born in 1730. He died in 1801 according to the Life Story of **Marie Angelique Choret** when he, **Charles Francois,** was about 70 years old. Place of death was in Lotbiniere, Quebec, Canada.

BEYOND FOURTH GREAT GRANDPARENTS

Fourth paternal great grandparents to **Ozema (Zem) LeDee**, and the seventh generation from where this chronicle began are **Angelique's** father, **Jacques "Charette" Choret** and **Marie Madeleine Chretien.** According to Ancestry Family Trees, **Jacques** was born in 1692 and **Marie Madeline** in 1699.

Jacques Choret's parents and fifth great grandparents to **Ozema LeDee** were **Pierre Choret** and **Marie Anne Baugis.** According to Family Search, the ancestral file database, **Marie Anne Baugis** was born on February 2, 1669 in Quebec, Canada. She was baptized at Notre Dame Cathedral in Quebec and was the daughter of **Madeline DuBois** and **Michael Baugis.**

Madeline DuBois born in 1640 died at the age of 81 in 1721. **Marie Anne's** father **Michael Baugis** was born in 1638 and died at the age of 79 in 1717. **Madeline** and **Michael** became parents to twelve children.

While **Marie Anne Baugis'** parents were **Madeline** and **Michael,** the parents of **Pierre Choret** were **Mathieu Choret** and **Sebastienne Veillon. Mathieu** and **Sebastienne** are therefore the sixth great grandparents to **Ozema LeDee**. **Mathieu** was born in 1624 and **Sebastienne** in 1628. **Mathieu Choret** lived to the approximate age of forty years, and his wife **Sebastienne** to age eighty.

A BRIEF SUMMATION

This report encompasses *nine generations* of genealogy investigation. Genealogical research is frequently conducted over a period of many years. This account is an investigation encompassing countless research and compilation hours exploring **Ozema LeDee's** family lineage. The researcher's goal was to gain knowledge of his progenitors and to have others hold dear to those who came before them.

Mistakes are inevitable, but the researcher/writer has made exhaustive efforts to avoid errors. It is the author's wish that the reader gain insight and understanding into the lives of their ancestors. Each claim represented is confirmed with documentation. Numerous other records can be invested to further explore the ancestors mentioned in this record. Investigating one's genealogy is a never-ending process.

A SYNOPSIS OF THE AREA INHABITATED BY THE LEDEE FAMILY

French and Spanish Territory

The land which became St. Landry Parish was inhabited since at least 10,500 B.C., as deduced from excavations of three prehistoric dwelling sites. By the 15th century, the Appalousa Indians settled in the area situated between the border of Texas-Louisiana.

The first European recorded in the Appalousa territory was a French trader named Michel de Birotte. He came in 1690 and negotiated with the Appalousa nation. Nine years later, France named Louisiana as a colony and defined the land occupied by the Appalousa as the Opelousas Territory. The area south of the Opelousas Territory was named Attakapas Territory.

In 1720 France established the Opelousas Post slightly north of the contemporary city of Opelousas. The post was a major trading organization for the developing area. France gave land grants to soldiers and settlers to encourage development. Most settlers were French immigrants.

Some Indians sold land to the newcomers. France yielded to Louisiana and its territories to Spain in 1762. Under Spanish rule, Opelousas Post became the center of government for Southwest Louisiana. By 1769 about 100 families were living in Opelousas Post. Between 1780 and 1820, the first settlers were joined by others coming from the Attakapas Territory. They were joined by immigrants from the French West Indies, who left after Haiti/St. Domingue became independent in a slave revolution. Most of the new settlers were French, Spaniards, French Creoles, Spanish Creoles, Africans and African Americans.

The group from Attakapas Post included many Acadians. These were French who migrated from Nova Scotia in 1763, after their expulsion by the English in the aftermath of France's defeat in the French and Indian War. On April 10, 1805, after the United States had acquired the Louisiana Purchase, the post was named the town of Opelousas and became the seat of the County of Opelousas. In 1807, when the territory was reorganized into parishes, Opelousas was designated the seat of St. Landry Parish.

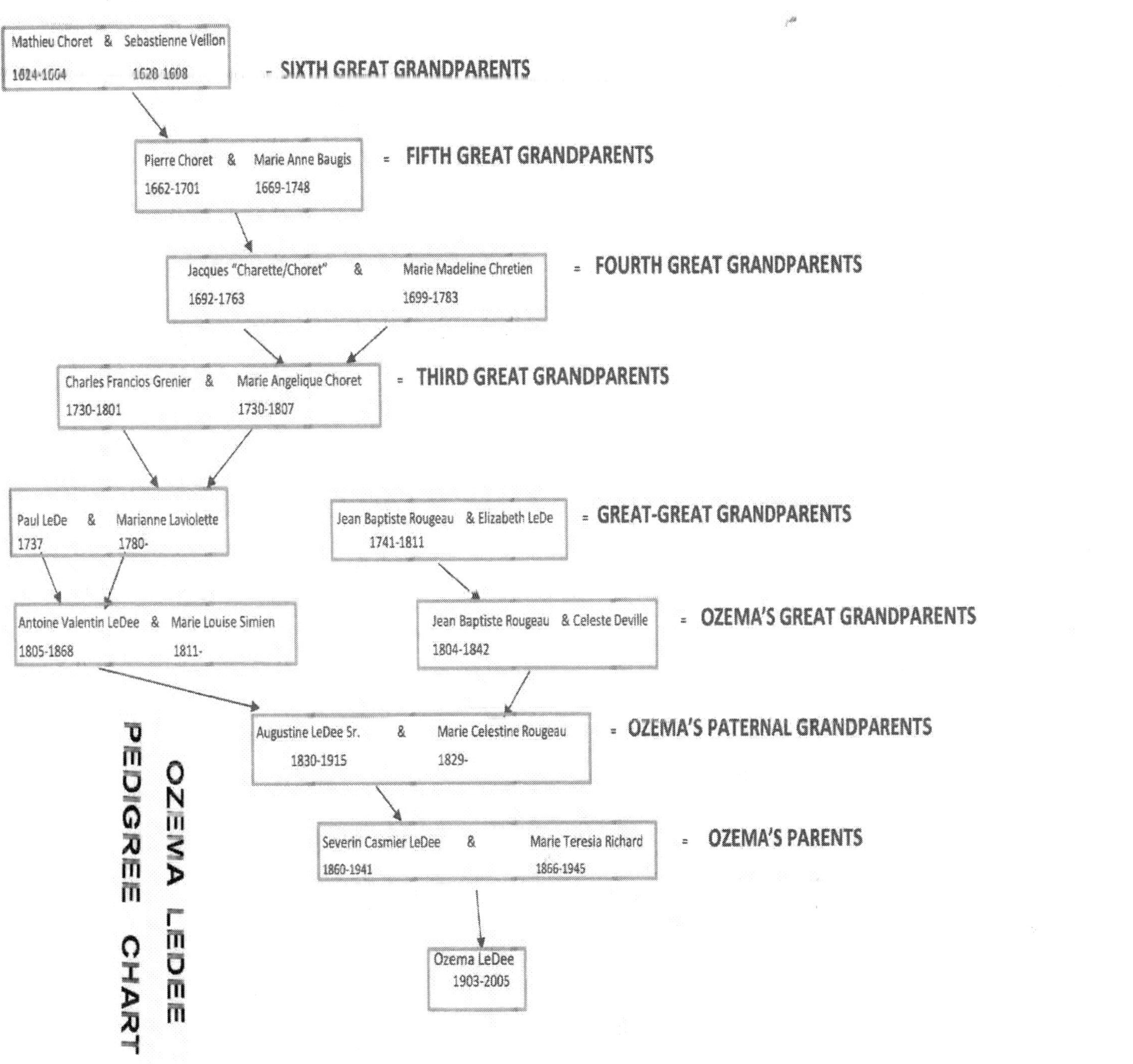
Mathieu Choret & Sebastienne Veillon
1624-1664 1620 1698
- SIXTH GREAT GRANDPARENTS
Pierre Choret & Marie Anne Baugis
1662-1701 1669-1748
= FIFTH GREAT GRANDPARENTS
Jacques "Charette/Choret" & Marie Madeline Chretien
1692-1763 1699-1783
= FOURTH GREAT GRANDPARENTS
Charles Francios Grenier & Marie Angelique Choret
1730-1801 1730-1807
= THIRD GREAT GRANDPARENTS
Paul LeDe & Marianne Laviolette
1737 1780-
Jean Baptiste Rougeau & Elizabeth LeDe
1741-1811
= GREAT-GREAT GRANDPARENTS
Antoine Valentin LeDee & Marie Louise Simien
1805-1868 1811-
Jean Baptiste Rougeau & Celeste Deville
1804-1842
= OZEMA'S GREAT GRANDPARENTS
Augustine LeDee Sr. & Marie Celestine Rougeau
1830-1915 1829-
= OZEMA'S PATERNAL GRANDPARENTS
Severin Casmier LeDee & Marie Teresia Richard
1860-1941 1866-1945
= OZEMA'S PARENTS
Ozema LeDee
1903-2005
OZEMA LEDEE
PEDIGREE CHART

ABOUT THE AUTHOR

Phyllis Pitre Lastrapes, M.A. is the oldest child of Ozeme's daughter, Leora Mae LeDee and her husband Paul V. Pitre. She has always delighted in hearing tales from her parents about their memories of their ancestors. When Phyllis entered her final year as an undergraduate student at Louisiana State University, her task was to determine a goal to complete by the end of the term. Back in 1989, her goal was to substantiate information she had learned through stories from her father and paternal grandmother about their lineage.

Thus, began Phyllis' quest with researching, compiling and writing family history. Although it has now been over 25 years since her first venture, the quest to research and write family history has not lessened. She has researched and written numerous genealogy chronicles and provided training sessions to groups whose desire has been to trace their own lineage.

Phyllis is the mother of two grown sons and has two grandchildren. Her passions are genealogy, travel, scrapbooking, and socializing with family and friends.

Ozeme LeDee

NOTES